To Stan

with best wishes

MEMORIES OF MR MOONLIGHT

FRANKIE
VAUGHAN

1. LASTING IMPRESSIONS
2. MR. SHOWBUSINESS
3. A LIFE CELEBRÉ

JIM FINN
2005

ISBN 0 9514040 8 3

Printed and bound by Crompton & Little
61a Linaker Street Southport PR8 5DQ.

Author's Note

This work is by no means intended to be a definitive study of the life of Frankie Vaughan, more a starting point to get his name back into the public domain and also provide the basis for a much larger volume at a later date.

Time

Time has all the treasures,

That time alone can bring

Give time to one another

Take time to laugh and sing

JIM FINN
2005

1.

FRANKIE VAUGHAN

Lasting Impressions

There is no doubt , not the slightest doubt whatsoever, no matter what anybody says, that Frankie Vaughan was the finest, greatest ambassador that Liverpool has ever had not only as a highly talented superstar but also as a truly wonderful person who endlessly cared and had time, time and even more time, for his fellow man, regardless of their social background, standing or religious belief.

Fellow Liverpudlian Jimmy Tarbuck, or "Sweet Lips" as Frankie affectionately called him, described Frank as the "most decent human being I've ever met in my life", a sentiment echoed by so many people up and down the country whose hearts were forever touched by his boundless energy, enthusiasm for, and genuine interest in, the lives of everyone he happened to meet.

Mike Henson, well known Lancashire comic, who regularly worked the Northern Club circuit for over three decades recalls the time he was the warm up comedian for top of the bill Frankie at Blighty's night club in Farnworth, near Bolton.

"Frankie was the most pleasant and friendliest person one could wish to meet. My eldest son, Peter, who was with the Army Bomb Disposal Squad in Northern Ireland in the early 1970's was home on leave at the time and he offered to drive me to Blighty's.

Arriving in the dressing room, Frankie was already there. He shook hands with me and my son and I explained to Frankie that Peter was at home on leave from Northern Ireland. A conversation between the two of them was struck up right away with Frankie showing a deep interest in the problems that people were experiencing over there.

I went on stage and 35 minutes later I concluded my act to find that they were still having the same discussion. The compere came in to the dressing room and asked Frankie if he could introduce him now. Frankie replied,

"Just give me a couple of minutes I am talking to Peter."

He even took the time to let my son take a picture of himself and me."

Frank's unremitting readiness and willingness to do good works for worthy causes whenever and wherever he could are well documented. Peter Pritchard, chairman of the Entertainment Artists' Benevolent Fund said of Frankie,

"Anytime we asked him to do us a favour it was always yes."

Sonny Warner MBE, highly regarded for his work around the hospitals and nursing homes in the Manchester area, and his wife Pam were very close friends of Frankie and Stella and regularly exchanged birthday greetings to one another. Sonny writes,

"Approximately 50 years ago my late brother emigrated to Portland, Oregon, USA. During his first two years he was working as a DJ Coast to Coast. The difference was, he decided to only present British bands and British artists. I became involved when he asked me to send records over to America with a short synopsis of each artist. This meant personally interviewing each artist to make it successful.

I arranged to meet Frankie Vaughan when he first appeared at the old Ardwick Hippodrome in Manchester and obtained his life story at first hand. We both hit it off immediately and became great friends – this was around 1952. Throughout the following years we corresponded regularly and whenever he was appearing in Manchester he made every effort to visit us and have a meal with us. We were also very friendly with his wife, Stella.

Whenever Frankie was in Blackpool, my wife, self and three young sons always paid him a visit. My eldest son, Brian, now runs the Lemon Tree Band and the Lemon Tree Theatrical Agency.

When Frankie passed away Stella invited us to the Memorial Service but as illness prevented me from going, we were represented there by two of our three sons.

It goes without saying that Frank was a real gentleman loved and admired wherever he went and the world is much poorer for his passing."

Basil Tait from Newquay, Cornwall, who was Frank's musical director between 1960 and 1968, and his wife Angela, had a chalet on the River Thames at Bourne End near Maidenhead. Basil recalls an amusing incident involving Frank,

"One summer Sunday afternoon Stella, Frank and their two children, David and Susan (it was before Andrew was born) came and spent the afternoon with us.

As the evening approached all on the river was quiet when suddenly we were aware of a radio blaring out from the opposite river bank. We looked up and could see a young couple settled down with their transistor radio with a programme we soon recognised as Radio Luxembourg, a station that was very popular in those days. Frank was furious and said,

"How can people ruin a glorious peaceful scene with music like that."

He asked me if I would take him over in the boat to tell them off as he didn't want to shout across. So I got the boat out and half way over we suddenly realised that the tune they were now playing was Frank's latest record!

When we got across the couple looked up and were amazed to recognise Frank who rather sheepishly said,

"Do you think you could possibly play that a little bit quieter, please?"

Over the years Frank attracted a huge following of loyal and devoted fans and he seemed to have the time for every single one of them.

In actual fact Frank considered every one of his fans to be a friend and his fan club was therefore known as "Frank and Friends". After his sad passing the name was changed to "Friends of Frank".

Secretaries Mrs. Edna Yeo and Mrs. Barbara Whitaker of the Nottingham and Derby branch provide us with just a few of their abiding memories.

"Frankie regarded all his genuine fans as friends and we have made so many lovely friends from all over the country all connected by the nicest man you could ever hope to meet and his family.

Frank was very proud of his charming wife, Stella, and as she supported him wholeheartedly and travelled with him to all his shows we were privileged to get to know her too as well as their children when they were able to be there.

We spent lots of happy memories of times travelling to and from different venues. One time we hired a minibus only to find the driver couldn't find his way from Nottingham to Peterborough! We arrived at the theatre at the interval luckily in time to see our Frank.

Frankie Vaughan was always so generous with his time. He never left after a show until every last autograph had been signed, every amateur had taken his or her last photograph and every lady went away thinking his smile was for her alone.

Some of the happiest days were when a tea party would be arranged for members of Frank and Friends and Stella and Frank would join us and chat to everyone before we all went to the show. The secretaries for the area concerned would be responsible for making the arrangements and we were always delighted when our turn came around.

One such occasion was when Frank was appearing at the Nottingham Theatre Royal. It was just after his 60th birthday and the party we held in the afternoon was a great success. Stella wasn't there as she was indulging in one of her favourite pastimes - shopping! Needless to say the show in the evening was superb, as always.

Another occasion we all gathered at a hotel in Birmingham for afternoon tea where Frankie was due to join us. Imagine our surprise when he arrived and told us that he had spent the day fishing. Not only had he caught a number of trout but the hotel chefs had cooked them and carried them in on trays held high to us for tea. Never has fish tasted so good."

Audrey Shannon, Secretary of the Preston and Blackpool branch of Friends of Frank recalls a time when Frank was at his most chivalrous.

"It was the summer of 1980 and Frank was hosting the Frankie Vaughan Golf Classic at the Hillside Golf Club, Southport, whilst starring in a summer season in Blackpool. Mary Woods, who was the then Preston and Blackpool secretary, and I went along taking my youngest daughter, Jill, who was seven years old. We had a lovely morning watching the celebrity golfers tee off and also being with Frank.

After our lunch in the club house, Mary and I discovered to our horror that Jill had disappeared. We looked everywhere for her and it was eventually suggested that we should call the police.

Unbeknown to Mary and me, Frank had taken a golf cart out on the course to look for Jill and had found her sat in a bunker chatting away to the comedian Russ Abbott.

He brought her back to us with Jill protesting that she wanted to follow Russ Abbott around the course!

That was just typical of the caring nature of the great man who I was proud to know and to call a friend and who we all still miss so much today."

Frankie Vaughan must have been born with a heart of gold. Right from an early age he demonstrated the caring side of his nature. His mother, Leah, recalled some years ago the time she had a clothing shop and Frank came in from school accompanied by one of his school friends who was wearing a rather shabby coat and a well worn out pair of trousers.

While she was busy with a customer, Frank helped himself to a bag from the shop and went upstairs. He re-appeared a few minutes later and handed the now bulky bag to his pal.

It was only later on when she found out he'd given his friend his own sports jacket and trousers.

"Frank loved to give," she said, "and when he gives, his very heart and soul are in it."

Frank spent a lifetime doing charitable work, raising thousands upon thousands of pounds for worthwhile causes and uplifting the spirits of countless numbers of people.

Caroline Fields from Arthington, West Yorkshire, writes,

"Frankie was my mother's favourite artiste so when he came to the Winter Gardens in Ilkley many years ago for a charity show my husband, John, and I took her along. It was a super show enhanced by the fact we had booked a box for a better view and had wined and dined on a superb supper – all served in our box, so we were really in the mood for parting with our cash!

The show was organised by a local estate agent Jimmy Horsley and compered by Andrew Sharpe, fellow estate agent and after dinner speaker, and amongst the supporting acts were the fabulous Acraloons. Then onto the floor came Frankie Vaughan who happened to look up to our box. He threw a kiss to my mum who nearly passed out. After two or three songs he asked for requests. These came at a high price as girls circulated the audience carrying small but seemingly bottomless wicker bowls. We filled in a request slip and handed over our money. My mum along with two dozen others had requested "Green Door" (as if he wouldn't have sung it anyway). A mini auction ensued as he shouted "Who shall I dedicate it to? Come on, who'll pay the highest price?" This happened with much of his programme that night and a great deal of money was raised for charity.

At the end of a wonderful show he moved in to the foyer where he asked for donations for a signed photograph. We formed an orderly queue and eventually reached the front. Frank searched absentmindedly for his pen whilst chatting to mum who, gooey eyed hung on his every word. She eventually realising what he was searching for, dug deep in her handbag and handed over her own pen.

She gave him £5 in return for a black and white photograph signed from him to her. After thanking him she put out her hand for the return of her pen. "Ah, so you'd like the pen as well. I lose so many that way," he laughed "Oh, all right then, give me a tenner and it's yours!"

And that is exactly what she did."

Joe Lynch from Meriden in the West Midlands tells a touching story,

"I had the great pleasure of meeting Frankie when he did his last Summer Season in Blackpool. He asked to meet my wife, Judy, and me to talk about doing a show for a mental heath charity. We had just lost our son, Simon, who sadly took his own life through mental illness. Judy and myself hoped to do some fund raising for the charity Simon was involved in.

Both Frankie and Stella met us backstage. They both showed such kindness. I broke down in tears. He said he would do the show for us. His agent, Peter Charlesworth who was always most kind, wrote to us. Sadly, Frankie became ill just after. The show never came off. My wife and I will never forget Frankie and Stella for their kindness to us in one of the saddest times in our life.

I am glad you are writing about one of the greatest showmen this country ever had and also the kindest human being one could wish to know."

A letter from Les Holt who works for the Jewish Telegraph in Manchester also highlights the unquestioned generosity of the great man.

"I first met Frankie Vaughan when he appeared at Manchester's Hulme Hippodrome. I managed to go backstage to meet him. I think it was his first professional appearance.

Several years later I was given his address and as I was running the London Marathon for a Jewish charity in Manchester I asked if he would sponsor me. I received a cheque for £100 in the return post. Somehow Frankie heard that the paper I was working for at the time, The Jewish Gazette (now defunct), was celebrating its 65th birthday – the same time as his. He sent me two lovely pictures of himself and his wife, Stella.

I spoke to him many times after that since he encouraged me to call him. He was always warm hearted, interested in myself and the paper. A great human being."

Iris Brandley writes from Nottingham.

"In the 1950's Frankie Vaughan came to Lowdham Street, Nottingham, to open the Russell Youth Club facing my grandad's pub the 'Plough and Harrow'. Everybody gathered outside. My grandad did a roaring trade that day.

When he arrived the street was packed solid. My mum was on the front row near to the door of the club. He came over to my mum, put his arm around her and kissed her hand.

It was a great day. My mum said she was never going to wash her hand again. She got a pair of surgical gloves and she wore this one glove for two weeks until it turned brown.

My dad wasn't very happy but it was my mum's great day. Her name was Ethel Wheat."

Further evidence if ever evidence were needed of Frankie's tireless and hectic lifestyle comes from Alice Kirkman, Derbyshire.

"Heanor, a small town in Derbyshire, used to hold an annual Victorian market on Bank Holiday Monday and in 1989 Frankie was asked to open it.

He came with his wife, Stella, and after opening the market he visited the Florence Shipley Home for Elderly People situated just off the market place.

My mother, Mrs Bertha Parker, was a resident there. She died in 1990 at the age of 99. Seeing Frankie was a great thrill for her as she was always a fan of his.

My mother was talking to Frankie when he called his wife over and said, "You had better come over here, Stella, I'm being chatted up."

I and my brother and my daughters were visiting mum at the time and found Frankie and his wife to be lovely people and really gave a big thrill to the elderly people in the home.

He is very sadly missed by so many people. He certainly touched our lives."

Another person was so impressed by the great man that he became a musician later on in life. Michael Tromp writes from Ormskirk.

"As a young boy in the 1950's I was taken to a garden fete at Pontville School, a school for underprivileged children which was to be opened by a 'famous celebrity'. The school was run by nuns and was for children whose parents, for some reason or another, couldn't look after them.

The 'famous celebrity' turned out to be Frankie Vaughan. He first appeared, flanked by two nuns, walking across the sports field towards a simple rostrum where there was a few chairs, a piano and a microphone.

Even as a child I was struck by this charismatic, sun tanned figure, immaculately dressed and looking like a million dollars. I recall his gleaming, crisp white shirt, perfectly ironed trousers and a blazer that looked like it had just come fresh from the tailors. He appeared to be a tall man with lots of hair and a very striking appearance. He really was an enigmatic figure.

After being introduced, he gave a speech with that 'laughing' voice about the good work being done at the school, encouraged people to part with their money for this good cause and then announced that due to contractual reasons he was not allowed to sing as he was appearing at a theatre in Lancashire and this prohibited him from singing within a 40 mile radius of the theatre. This brought a huge combined sigh from the crowd.

He then said, "If I don't tell anyone, promise me you won't." A huge cheer followed and his pianist stepped up to an old upright piano on the rostrum.

Frankie then broke into 'Little Things Mean A Lot'. It was my first taste of live music and of seeing a real live 'pop' star, a huge thrill for me as well as the crowd. He sang one more song before he left for a 'pressing engagement'. I never forgot that larger than life appearance from a nice, charming showbiz star.

Later on in life I became a musician and it was this performance that kick started my interest in music."

It is uncanny that Frankie Vaughan was a very ordinary man but with very special qualities and an extraordinary ability to make very ordinary people feel very, very special. He certainly made the day for Marian Costin from Stockport in Cheshire.

"I worked in Debenham's restaurant and I got the chance to see him when he made a visit to the store. I was near to where he was sitting and when he had finished with his tea tray he turned to me and said, "Who will move this?" Thrilled at the chance to speak to him I said, "I will, Mr. Vaughan." I took the tray and he smiled just for me. It was wonderful.

If stars are in heaven he is the brightest. Loved by thousands not just as a singer but also a youth icon especially in Liverpool. What a man and what a loss to entertainment".

Margaret Cooper from Nottingham also has a nice story to tell.

"I met Frankie in Woolworth's, Nottingham, when he was selling his album. I bought it and he signed it for me. I thought it was wonderful for him to do that. A few years passed and I still thought he was great.

Later on when I became a widow I took in a student and we seemed to get on very well. One Friday afternoon I came home to find my student was with a nice young man and she introduced him to me. Lo and behold! It was Frankie Vaughan's son, Andy. I really thought I was going to pass out. He was at college with my student.

After that I saw a lot of him, by then he was 21. His dad had bought him a car. It was a pleasure to have him here.

It upset me very much when Frankie was taken ill in the John Radcliffe Hospital, Oxford, where he died. It was so sad.

I sent his wife, Stella, a sympathy card and she sent me a lovely letter back. I shall treasure it. There will never be another like Frankie. Bless him."

Eileen Woods from Bourneville, Birmingham, has never forgotten the time she gazed upon the most handsome man she had ever seen.

"Back in 1952 we still had trams in Birmingham and I worked in a shop in town. In those days Wednesday was half day closing.

One Wednesday afternoon I was on the tram sitting on a side seat, there were straps above for persons standing.

Going along Bristol Street a young man got on. He didn't bother to sit down. He stood in front of me hanging on to one of the straps. I looked up into the most handsome, beautiful face I had ever seen. I looked away but to make sure I wasn't dreaming I looked again and he smiled at me. I just melted. He only went two or three stops and then got off. I couldn't get his face out of my mind.

That same night I went to the Hippodrome with my new boy friend and they announced a new singing sensation. Yes – it was Frankie Vaughan. I couldn't believe it. I shouted at the top of my voice, "It's him. It's the chap on the tram".

I am 75 years of age now and I still treasure that memory."

Brian McNally of Low Fell in Gateshead, tells of the time Frankie had lost his voice but was still able to turn on his magical charm.

"In October 1976, despite being really ill with his throat, Frankie Vaughan came to the Central Social Club in Gateshead to present a cheque to the children of St Vincent's Orphanage.

After he had presented the cheque, which was an awful lot of money for the children of the orphanage, everybody went wild and shouted for him to sing. His manager shook his head and poor Frankie had an anxious look on his face. Then Brenda Bell shouted from the audience, "Frankie, if you can't give us a song then give us a kick," and Frankie gave one of his famous kicks to cheers of delight. This got Frankie 'off the hook' and everybody was happy. Frankie then went off to another engagement in Newcastle.

How many times Frankie gave his time for others must be many. We still talk about him and we think the world of him. Liverpool must be proud of having such a good son as

Frankie Vaughan. He was the salt of the earth."

Christey Robertson-Glasgow from Bath in Somerset entertains us with another interesting story about Frankie.

"In the year 1956 I took a French girl, Beatrice and my friend, Kate, to Bristol to see Frankie. Beatrice had "Frankie" and I had "Vaughan' printed on our tee shirts.

After the show we went round to the stage door and the doorman let us in. We saw Frankie and had a conversation with him. I pretended to be French and Kate translated to him. I said it was late and that we were going to find it difficult to get home. He said, generously, that he would get his chauffeur to take us home after he had been dropped off.

We climbed into this huge car and off we went with Frankie. After the chauffeur had taken us safely back home we had a fantastic laugh.

My brother produces chickens and for several years to come I sent a chicken to Frankie on his birthday.

Years later I saw him in a show in London. He was wearing a tartan dressing gown. He thanked me for sending the chickens."

Mrs. Joyce Toon of Kings Norton in Birmingham has been a devoted fan of Frankie since the early 1950's.

" I loved Frankie Vaughan. He was a very caring, unselfish man and a great entertainer, also a lovely family man.

I have many happy memories of going around the country to see him at clubs and theatres. One particularly stands out.

Myself and five friends went to see him at the 'Night Out' in Birmingham. My friend, Sadie, drove us there in her large Humber. We couldn't stay to see him after the show as we had to get home. He was always brilliant in coming out after his shows to greet and sign photos for his fans.

Anyway, we went and got the car and just as we were passing the 'Night Out', who did we see just getting into a taxi but Frankie and Stella.

We all shouted to Sadie to follow that taxi. We sped round an island, tyres screeching. We didn't need to go very far as the taxi pulled up outside a Chinese restaurant. As they got out of the taxi we all jumped out of our car and ran to him. His comment was. "Where have you all come from?" We told him. He really laughed and was his usual gentleman self.

We decided not to hassle him anymore and all of us kissed him goodnight. We went home very happy.

I've got lots of photos, cuttings and magazines and of course all his records. I shall keep them till I die. I have told the family to bury them with me. I have many pictures on the walls in my shop which have always started many a conversation.

I had my first LP and record player bought for me by my brother when I was about 13 years old.

When I lived at home my mother played the piano and used to have all the family photos on top plus one of Frankie. People used to ask why it was there and I would reply that he was one of the family.

Show business lost a great entertainer. His wife, Stella, who was also a very pleasant woman, lost a loving husband, his family lost a loving father and grandfather and his loyal fans lost a genuinely caring man."

The expression 'you cannot please all the people all of the time' goes hand in glove with a similar expression 'you cannot be all things to all people.' Well, that may be so but I am sure Frankie Vaughan is the closest anybody has got to it. His warmth as a person and his talent as a showbusiness personality have earned him the love, affection and admiration of so many people right throughout his long and illustrious career.

Mr. J. D. Wiseman of Grimsby tells of the time his wife sat through one of Frankie's shows nursing a broken foot.

"In 1974 Frankie was appearing at Bunny's Club in Cleethorpes. My wife, a devoted fan of his, had borrowed my daughter's high heel shoes to finish off her outfit.

In her excitement at going to see Frankie and not being all that used to the shoes, unbeknown to us she had toppled over and injured her foot.

31

She didn't say anything to us about this and sat through the show as if everything was all right.

After the show was over she told us what had happened and asked to be taken to A. & E. for an x-ray and it was discovered that she had a broken bone in her foot.

Truly a star performance by one of his biggest fans."

Sheila Beaumont of Louth in Lincolnshire remembers seeing Frankie in Grimsby some years ago.

"I saw Frankie Vaughan, I think it was about seven years ago at the Grimsby Auditorium. It was just wonderful seeing and listening to him.

After the show we were told if we waited 15 minutes we could speak to him. I, of course, waited with about 30 others. I was nearly the last one to get to him. The other ladies were kissing him. I would have loved to but I didn't think it was fair to expect him to kiss so many ladies. Instead, when it was my turn I shook his hand and said, "I would like to wish you good health." He held my hand for a while and then said thoughtfully, "It is the best thing you could wish for me."

I could weep writing this down. He was a wonderful man. He had done so much good for needy young people and was a wonderful entertainer".

During his career, Frankie was called upon to do some unusual things in the name of charity and Mrs. Dorothy Campion of Arnold in Nottingham, describes one such occasion.

"As you know Frankie supported the boys' clubs and 40 years ago in 1964, there was great excitement when we found out he was to visit our boys' club, the William Olds Boys' Club.

Frankie acted as the caller for the bingo and much to my delight I won. Everyone, including Frankie, had a great laugh when he presented me with my prize, a marrow!"

Mrs. June Spencer of Gedling in Nottingham was thrilled when she met Frank in Woolworths.

"I met Frankie in Woolworths when he was promoting his double album, '100 Golden Greats' there. He actually spoke to me and asked me my name. I froze on the spot. He had to ask me again. I told him 'June' and he signed the album. 'To June with Love'. I will never forget that moment. He was my idol. No other singer comes close to him."

However, when Frankie started to hit the headlines early in his career as the newest singing sensation there was one lady who was totally unaware of his growing popularity. David Morris of Louth in Lincolnshire recalls an amusing incident.

"I was a student at Leeds College of Art in the 1950's after Frankie had left to pursue his show business career and he was already very well known. The story could well be apocryphal but it was commonly reported that he came back to the college on a 'state visit'.

The students were well aware of his status in the pop world and he was subjected to a degree of fan worship but not by everybody.

Miss Auty was the member of staff who taught plant drawing in the attic at the top of the building and she was a rather timid lady who had some problems persuading the young male students to concentrate on her subject.

When she happened to meet Frankie she was reported to have said, "Oh! Hello Abelson, and how are you getting on now?"

She had no idea of course, of the pop singer's fame."

In actual fact there was one particular person who was not very impressed at all. Mr. Arthur Cairns from Dalmarnock, Glasgow, writes,

"I first met Frankie Abelson in the Army in 1947 when we were in Egypt with the Royal Army Medical Corps. He was always with his three Liverpool pals. We were all in the same billet.

Then one day he moved out. He told us he was doing a different job working for a new Medical Officer.

After that we saw very little of him. He never came back to the NAAFI."

Two fellow Glaswegians have a different tale to tell. Mary Dawson of East Kilbride says,

" I had the pleasure of meeting Mr. Moonlight at the Empire stage door when he came to

Glasgow. He was very charming and gave me his autograph. We had a few minutes talk and he wished me well."

That memory is as fresh in her mind now as it was then. Mary is still so excited by it all that she asked if she could be mentioned in the book. Mary, done!

Renee Max from Langside, Glasgow, was also delighted to have met Frank. He knew Frank for about 43 years from when he first appeared at the Glasgow Empire and they became good friends with each other.

In the '50's and '60's many major British cities suffered from rival gangs battling it out on the streets using such offensive weapons as broken bottles, knives, bicycle chains and leather studded belts striking fear into the very hearts of law abiding people right across the country.

Because a great deal of respect was accorded to Frankie Vaughan by young people everywhere as the result of his tireless efforts over a long period to raise money for the Boys' Clubs movement, he was invited by the powers that be to join a committee to discuss ways of bringing this juvenile delinquency to an end.

Glasgow was particularly affected by this inter gang warfare and it ended up with Frankie going to Glasgow and meeting up with several members of these various gangs face to face, pointing out to them the errors of their ways and actually persuading them to hand in their weapons to the police.

Such was the stature of the man in the eyes of the youth of yesteryear.

Mr. I. J. Robinson of Leeds was a young offender in the 1950's in the Aigburth area of Liverpool.

"I recall the year 1953/54, when I was 15 years of age and Frankie did a lot of good work for the youth of the Dingle and the area thereabouts. It was well noted throughout the whole of Liverpool at the time.

Lads of my age always had a lot of respect for him.

I used to be in the Merchant Navy with Alfred Holt and Company, the Blue Funnel Line, and I met lads from all over Liverpool and Birkenhead who had the greatest respect for him. I hope I have thrown some light on the work he did which a lot of people don't know about. He was also a great entertainer."

Brian Young from St Ann's in Nottingham, along with all his pals, had every reason to be grateful to Frankie when they were stationed in the Far East with the Army.

"I remember in the early seventies, can't remember exactly what year, I was at the time a young soldier, I must have been about 21 years of age, serving in H.M. forces in Hong Kong. My regiment was the 47 Light Regiment, Royal Artillery.

One day our sergeant came into the barrack room and announced that Frankie Vaughan was coming to visit our camp to sing us a few of his famous songs. Of course, we thought it was a wind up, but it wasn't.

A hastily arranged stage was set up in our gun sheds and although it was really outside there was a corrugated roof overhead with about 30 or more chairs in place.

It seems that Frankie was on his way to Australia and had stopped in Hong Kong in between connections. Because he had a few hours spare he offered to do a free concert for us.

When he first arrived we all stood up to greet him. He had his hat and his cane and started off with 'Give Me The Moonlight'. He must have done an hour at least and sang all his favourites. I was near the front and only yards away from him but alas never got the chance to get his autograph.

I mean I was a young soldier and never a great fan of his but I will never forget the experience. He was as good as gold and before he said goodbye he thanked us all for a very good welcome. He was then whisked away to continue on his way.

He was a true gent and of course did it for us for nothing. I'm not sure if he sang for other units in Hong Kong but he couldn't have had too much time during his stopover. I was pleased he came, as was everybody else. A true star in my eyes. I remember we gave him a standing ovation at the end although I am quite sure he was well used to that.

Our camp was actually miles away from Hong Kong's airport and hotels so he must have gone to a lot of trouble to entertain us. I have always admired him after that for the entertainment he provided for me and my army pals that day. Everytime afterwards I saw him on television or in the news I remembered the effort that he made to make us happy.

Frankie was a fine man and singer. His wife must be proud of him. I had respect for him.

Thank you, Frankie Vaughan. Rest in peace."

From October 1962 until July 1963 I lived in the sleepy village of Endmoor, Westmoreland as it was then, Cumbria now, four miles south of Kendal, one mile or so from Oxenholme railway station, which incidentally is the same village that Frankie was evacuated to during the Second World War, before moving on to the city of Lancaster. I was on a course at the time at Summerlands Furniture Company training to be a wood machinist, not that I had any ambition to be a wood machinist, but I had only recently come out of the Merchant Navy and I needed something to do whilst I contemplated my future.

On my return to Liverpool I got a job in the Meccano toy factory where they made train sets, Dinky toys and Meccano kits. There was a 'no smoking' policy throughout the entire factory but members of staff used to congregate for a smoke in the tiny toilet areas where the air would be that thick with cigarette smoke you could cut it with a knife.

Just a few weeks before Christmas in 1963, Frankie Vaughan made a visit to the factory to pay for a consignment of toys for underprivileged children and whilst he was being entertained by senior management he was invited to have a tour around the factory which he duly accepted.

When he entered, with his entourage, the main assembly room, which comprised mainly female labour, he was recognised by some of the women who immediately downed tools and ran towards him. Everybody else then stopped work and the conveyor belts came to a sudden halt. In no time Frankie was surrounded by swooning girls reaching out to touch him. The supervisory staff had to fend them off. Eventually some kind of order was restored enabling Frankie to quietly leave the building and everything returned to normal.

I was in the smoke filled Gent's toilet along with other members of staff drawing heavily on the dreaded weed when the Production

Manager came dashing in, fumbling nervously in his pockets for his lighter and cigarettes. His hair was tousled, one side of his white overall was pulled off his shoulder and his tie was pulled away from his collar. Normally he stood tall and proud. A calm and collected Scot. Now he was dishevelled and couldn't wait to get the cigarette into his mouth. He took one exasperated puff of his cigarette and as he blew out the smoke he drawled in his 'Sean Connery' accent, "I'd like to know where it says in my contract that part of my job is to pull screaming women off famous pop stars." He did, however, have a pleasurable smile on his face.

A little known fact about Frankie, so little known in fact, that I doubt if even Frankie himself knew about it, was his apparent ability to quieten overly loquacious mothers-in-law. I explain.

In the 1970's when I lived with my then wife in Skelmersdale, Lancashire, her mother came to spend a couple of weeks during the summer with us, as was her wont and custom, and I just didn't know how I was going to get through with it. If there were international talking contests, my mother-in-law would have been world champion. From first thing in the morning till last thing at night her tongue never stopped.

After having my ear bent non stop for the best part of two days I decided to take both of them to see Frankie at the Southport Theatre. I was hoping that she would stay quiet long enough for me to enjoy the show which fortunately she did.

When the show was over, we repaired to the lounge bar for a drink before setting off home. When I returned to the table with the tray of drinks, my mother-in-law looked rather sheepish. She was all starry eyed and fervently wrapping the hem of her dress more and more tightly around her forefinger. I couldn't get a word out of her.

Apparently Frankie had walked through the lounge whilst I was at the bar and had spoken to her. She just couldn't believe it. The man himself asking her how she enjoyed the show.

She never spoke in the car all the way back home. In fact, she hardly spoke very much for the rest of her holiday. She spent most of her time sitting in her arm chair gazing and smiling into space with that 'oh so far away' look on her face.

Thanks, Frank.

Whilst we're on about Skelmersdale, the home town of Doris Steele, well known jazz singer who has sung with many of the top London bands including Nat Temple, recounts the time she worked with Frankie in the late 1960's.

"I was on a show on Radio Luxembourg called 'The Marilyn Programme' and I did a song with him entitled 'My Heart Stood Still'. He was also with the same dance band as I was, with Nat Temple, but at different times.

Nat Temple for some reason fell out with Frank, therefore, when I knew I was going to do a duet with him I was worried but he was charming and brought me a cup of coffee during the break. We contacted each other on the phone later concerning work. I found him to be an interesting person and very proud of coming from Merseyside."

And what better way to conclude the first section of the book than by including a contribution from the beautiful Isle of Man.

Janice Cottier from Onchan, writes,

"When our daughters were young we stayed in the small African country called Lesotho, formerly known as Basutoland. It was not very often that a suitable show came to the Holiday Inn that we could take them to see.

One day it was announced that Frankie Vaughan was coming to perform a cabaret and we enquired as to the suitability of taking the girls to it. The management assured us it was all right for the family so we duly went and thoroughly enjoyed the performance.

Things were going so well that at the end of the show, feeling very pleased, we decided to have a nightcap, then the fun began. Without any warning the next act came on.

A stripper!! Our oldest daughter's eyes came out on stalks. "Why is that lady wearing night clothes?" and "Why is she letting that man untie the ribbons on her gown?"

We bid a hasty retreat. Unfortunately we had very good seats right at the front of the audience and our progress to the exit was in full view of everyone there.

Over the ten years we lived there, we saw many more good shows - Tommy Trinder came for a few weeks. We were always very careful to check up on the supporting artistes before we took the girls again!!"

All part of life's rich tapestry into which is woven the wonderful and colourful world of showbusiness.

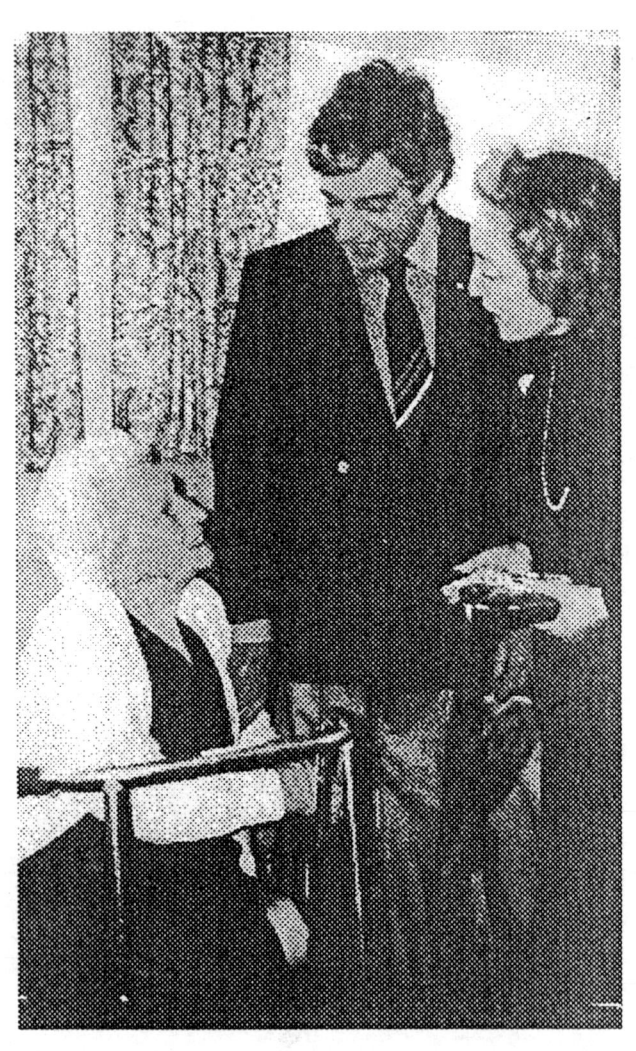

Frank and Stella with Mrs Bertha Parker

Frank with Sonny Warner

Frank with Audrey Shannon on his left and Chris Lester

Frankie Vaughan o.s.s.   19th February, 1993.

My dear Sonny,

Many happy returns for your 70th birthday.
I can't believe it.   We go back so many
years, you and Pam and Stella and me.   It
was such a delight to make your acquaintance
once again in Blackpool, let's hope we can
keep in touch.

Your brother Barney gave me an invitation.
Maybe one of these days we can take him up
on it when I am better.

Nice to see you are working so hard up in
Manchester in your very caring way around
the hospitals and nursing homes.   You are
doing a very good job.

Fondest love from Stella,

Regards,

Frank.

Frankie Vaughan O.B.E.   13th November, 1992.

My dear Sonny and Pamela,

I thank you so much for your kind letter and
good wishes.

Yes, I am making progress now, thank goodness.
It was a terrible shock, but then again let's
face it, I have been very lucky and with the
help of my darling wife, loving family and
friends, I will be back to normal, please God
in the Spring.

Please give your brother, Barney, and his wife
Rose all our fondest love. We enjoyed meeting
them.

Much success and congratulations on the good
work you are doing in Manchester.

Stella joins me in sending all our love to
you and yours,

Frank.

Frank with Mike Henson

Frank with Sonny Warner

FRANKIE VAUGHAN
(Baritone Vocalist)

DESCRIPTION   - Extremely good looking, swarthy, black
haired young Yorkshire man of Greek/Jewish appearance
rather like Victor Mature. In light blue suit and bow tie.

DATE   - 11 October 1953

PERFORMANCE   - Too Young
                 Shangai
                 My Desire
                 Jezebel

EXPERIENCE   - One year music hall experience. Currently
with Nat Temple.

REMARKS   - Twisted lip movement in slow numbers and
marked tremolo which may be due to nerves. Has natural
small volumed light baritone voice. Well suited to the
mike. Personal magnetism and a certain cave mannish charm
which would certainly register with most people and appeal
to most women. Should prove suitable for TV solo spot
with a light production. Also has exaggerated tricks of
showmanship.

2.

FRANKIE VAUGHAN

Mr.
Showbusiness

In the 1950's, most of those in their early teens joined one or other of the several youth organisations prevalent at the time just as Frankie got himself involved with the Boys' Club in Lancaster in the 1940's.

The main advantage of such organisations was that young people had a range of character building activities to choose from as part of their ongoing personal development as well as helping to keep them off the streets and possibly ending up on the wrong side of the law.

In 1954 I joined the 22nd Liverpool Company of the Boys' Brigade and one of the highlights was the annual camp held in the Isle of Man.

I remember in 1957 we were billeted in a school in St. John and we heard that there was a film about Liverpool showing at the cinema in Peel and so we all trooped off to see it. It was called 'These Dangerous Years'.

I was totally fascinated by the scenes of Liverpool being displayed upon the screen but when Frankie appeared I couldn't believe my eyes. I was so astonished by the charisma of his larger than life personality that I wandered down the aisle at the side of the auditorium in order to get a closer look and stood there until the usher came down and ordered me back to my seat. From that point on my admiration for the man was set in stone and never diminished as years went by.

Frankie made several films during his career in showbusiness including one with Arthur Askey curiously called "Ramsbottom Rides Again." I never saw this film but I can imagine it to have been a tremendous 'hoot'.

The icing on the cake of course had to be when Frankie played opposite the legendary world's most sexiest woman, Marilyn Monroe, in 1960. The film was entitled "Let's Make Love", which was all very well but when Marilyn wanted to re-enact the scenes with Frankie 'off the set', that is where he decided to draw the line and pass that one up. His love was entirely for his wife, Stella, and for his family and that virtually put an end to what would certainly have been a fabulous Hollywood stardom for him.

Frankie often said that he treasured his family life more than anything else, including his professional life, and that was where his main priorities lay.

Dr. Eileen Gillespie of Nottingham can very well vouch for that.

"In the summer of 1957 I was a newly qualified Junior House Officer working on a children's ward in Leeds. We heard rumours that an epidemic of Asian 'Flu was about to erupt but senior staff were very sceptical. However, they were wrong and because I was one of the youngest members of staff and had had less time to build up any immunity, I was one of the first to succumb. The advantage of this was that by the time the epidemic really took hold, I was fully recovered and could experience all the problems that followed.

By September the country was in its grip. The number of admissions soared but also more and more medical staff and ambulance crews were falling victim to the epidemic.

On one evening two severely ill girls from two separate addresses arrived in one ambulance. We could see they were more ill than any of the other 'flu admissions and we wondered if they would survive.

A few days later I was asked if the uncle of one of these girls could visit - a rather unusual request I thought but raised no objection. Then later I was told he would be arriving at 1.00 am! This really was strange. Uncles don't usually ask permission to visit but at 1.00 am, it was unheard of. However, we were working all hours anyway so we acceded to his request.

Only later did I discover that the uncle in question was Frankie Vaughan and his late arrival was probably due to having to travel a considerable distance from where he was on tour at the time. The fact that he did and his manner showed the caring side of his nature.

We were all relieved when his niece, I think her name was Linda Shock, eventually made a full recovery.

My only sadness was that one of the junior nurses asked him for his autograph as he departed. It did not seem the appropriate time for that, but despite his obvious concern for his niece he signed the piece of paper she thrust before him and graciously went on his way."

In an interview several years ago, Frankie's mother, Leah, described the time he came to see her before setting off to America.

Leah lived in a flat in Leeds which Frank had bought for her and he happened to remark how cold it was in the hallway. Before he left he told his mother to have a radiator fitted before the winter set in and he would organise for his accountant to settle the bill.

As soon as he arrived back home from Las Vegas having been away for all of six months he contacted his mother and asked if she had got the radiator fitted in the hall. She had to confess that she hadn't. She felt as though she had had more than enough from Frankie. True, Frankie had made a lot of money over the years but she knew that he had given a lot of it away sometimes without anybody knowing about it and he wasn't as rich as many people believed. As long as his family and his children were happy then to him that was more important than all the money in the world.

I suspect that making films was not really Frank's cup of tea and he did not regret turning his back on a bright and certain future in the glamorous Hollywood film industry.

Frank's wholesome stage presence and unique brand of star quality made him a natural for playing to live audiences whether he was on the theatre or in cabaret in the restaurants and clubs.

His friendly rapport with his audience was very much a consistent feature and highlight of his act and he had that special 'something' of being able to make everybody, especially the women, feel warmly welcome and every inch a part of the show.

As a performer, Frankie Vaughan was the consummate professional, his timing faultless, always immaculately dressed, his craftsmanship honed to perfection by his artistic use of the many trade marks he adopted as his very own - the top hat and tails, boater, the giggle in his voice, the twirl of a cane and of course, his famous high kick.

Quite often, when Frankie was part way through his signature tune, "Give Me The Moonlight," which he chanced upon in a back street shop in Glasgow, he would stroll leisurely to the side of the stage, cane under his arm, look over his right shoulder, stop, fix his smile on one lucky female, give her a teasing wink of his eye, jerk his head for her to follow him and then continue with his stroll towards the wings. Absolute poetry in motion!

Sheila More from Cotgrave in Nottingham tells us of the time she nearly became the proud owner of a Frankie Vaughan cane.

"I went to see Frankie in the 1950's at the Empire in Nottingham. I went four nights on the trot one week. It was when he was just starting his career.

At the side of the Empire there was a little 'jitty' where the stars would come out to sign autographs. There used to be a man on the door whose job it was to keep the fans in order but this particular night no one was there. Only all of us fans waiting to see our idol.

I took my chance and sneaked in. I found Frankie's dressing room and it was empty. In there I saw his cane which he used especially for his song, "Give Me The Moonlight", but before I could take it, I'm afraid I got caught by Frankie himself.

What a gentleman he was. He started to laugh and said, "What would I do without my cane for my act on stage?" He didn't tell me off. He just joked about it and gave me a pencil instead. What a marvellous man he was to talk to.

If I had got that cane it would be worth something today. Never mind, I tried, and I have my memory of meeting and talking with Frank which will remain with me forever."

Arthur Booth of Liverpool, went to see one of Frankie's shows on medical advice.

"I have multiple sclerosis and receive physiotherapy to help with my mobility. A few years ago my physiotherapist said that I should try to get my leg higher. I told her I was going to see Frankie Vaughan and so would have a good teacher when he did his high kicks. We arrived at Bodelwyddan Castle and saw Frankie and Stella walking from the car park.

After dinner we settled down to watch the show and when Frank appeared almost the first thing he said was that he was unable to do his high kicks as he had had an operation on his knee.

He gave a wonderful performance and at the end he said he would like to meet as many people as possible in the reception area. My sister in law ran out to join the queue and when she got near to the front I was taken to join her in my wheelchair.

When I reached Frankie I thanked him for a wonderful show but said, "talk about ever been had" and I went on to tell him about my physiotherapist and the high kicks and then him announcing that he wasn't able to do them.

He looked at me for a few seconds then said with a smile, "You come from Liverpool, don't you? With a sense of humour like that you can only come from Liverpool."

We had a laugh and then I had to move on whilst my sister in law spoke to him. It was a most memorable night."

Mrs. Averill Samm of Newburgh in Lancashire has a story about one of Frankie's straw boaters.

"In the late 1950's, myself and three friends who were great fans of Frankie, were going to the London Palladium to see him. At the time I was living in Luton which was the main town for hat manufacturing.

A few days before the show we asked one of the hat factories if they could make us a straw boater to take with us to give to Frankie. They finished it with about an hour to spare before we had to catch our train. They put 'Made Specially for Frankie Vaughan' in gold lettering on the white satin lining.

We were invited into his dressing room to give it to him and to have our photos taken with him. He wore that hat during his performance.

It was a great day and he was really nice. I still have the photos safely put away to this day."

If Frankie Vaughan wasn't a born romantic then he certainly became an incurable romantic at a later date. His looks, style and panache would have made any woman go weak at the knees.

True, Frankie was considered by some to be an irrepressible flirt, particularly on stage, but everybody, including his wife, Stella, knew it was really only a bit of fun as part of his act and he didn't mean anything by it at all.

Frankie met Stella at the Mecca Locarno ballroom in Leeds in 1949 and after a dance or two and a cup of tea, he took her home on the tram and that very night asked her to be his girl forever. And that was it. Stella became his greatest pleasure in life. Even when he was ill in hospital for the last time he still arranged for a bunch of roses to be presented to her on the occasion of their wedding anniversary which was something he had done through their entire married life.

Frank was always very comfortable with the ladies. He was an only son with three younger sisters. He was brought up mainly by his grandmother because his parents had to work long and hard in order to make ends meet. Stella also had three sisters who were very close to their grandmother and so Frankie had a ready made fan club right from the very start.

This probably accounts for the ease with which he was able to conduct an abstract, tongue-in-cheek, 'love affair' with any of the girls who made up the core of most of his audiences and quite often he would tease one of his unsuspecting, adoring fans to come up and join him on stage.

Mrs. Susan Wiley from Sidmouth in Devon,

"I have been a fan of Frank's since the age of 12 years and my parents always took me to see him if he was doing a concert around my birthday in May.

This particular year, my 16th birthday, Frank was topping the bill at the London Palladium so we duly went along and sat in the front row of the stalls.

When Frank came on he asked if anyone had a birthday. I put up my arm and he invited me onto the stage and danced and sang to me.

I was on 'Cloud Nine' and finished up with some of his stage make up on my cheek which stayed there until it wore off. He also gave me a box of beautiful chocolates to take home.

When I saw him some ten years ago I reminded him of this and we had a good laugh about it.

My mother would always stand with me at the stage door where Frank was appearing waiting for his autograph. We had some good times and both my husband and I felt it was a great privilege to have met him as a friend at one of the Warner's get togethers.

He was a real friend as well as a great star."

Mrs. Renee Minton, Cyncoed, Cardiff, had a very similar experience.

"I have always been a fan of Frankie Vaughan since I was a teenager. My first really big moment was in 1957 when I was just 16 years old.

Frankie was doing a show at the London Palladium and my two friends and myself got front row tickets numbers 1, 2 and 3, knowing that he always chose someone from that part of the audience to speak to. We paid 16 shillings (80p in today's money) per ticket which was a lot of money then.

During the show, as expected, he came down and "Yes" chose me to go back on to the stage with him to sing to. The song was "Am I Wasting My Time". Part way through the song he asked me my age and when I said 16, he walked up the stage still singing and left me on my own in the middle of the stage. I just stood there and waited until he came back. He then kissed me on the cheek and took me back to my seat. It was a fabulous moment which I will never forget.

In between the years I saw him dozens of times at different places and always spoke to him and he always remembered me.

In 1979 he was doing a cabaret in Cardiff for our Jewish wives group of which I was the secretary. I had of course put myself and my husband on the table just in front of him on stage but very unfortunately, three weeks before the show, I lost my father and so could not go.

When Frank arrived at the house of a friend of mine before the show, he was told I was not going to be there and why. He then telephoned my house to speak to me to give his condolences regarding my dad but I was not there – I had gone to see my mum in Reading.

My husband, Phill, took the call and told me when I got home. I could have cried. I was so disappointed but I did write to him to thank him.

I saw him a few times after that and thanked him again. I was really devastated when he died. He was a lovely man and I really do miss him."

Mrs. A. Bontoff of Grimsby, recounts the time when Frankie called her and five of her friends onto the stage.

"I was a great fan of Frankie and still am. I have a picture of him and me together and pictures of him all over my home. My husband says it's all Frankie and not one of him.

I loved Frankie very much and went all over the country to see him. When I was a member of his fan club we went to his 70th birthday party and we bought him a golf club.

When he came to Grimsby I went on stage and sang "Give Me The Moonlight" with him. Before he sang "Green Door" he told us he had had a knee operation and wouldn't be able to kick up his leg and so six of us went up on stage and cocked up our legs for him.

I used to work in a factory and when one of the girls said Frankie was rubbish I punched her. Nobody ever called him again. After that, when I entered the factory, all the girls used to sing "Give Me The Moonlight".

Frankie will always be my Mr. Moonlight".

Frank first started singing at the age of 11 years when he was with the Synagogue choir, Princes Road, Liverpool, from where he probably began to develop the strong, emotional feel he had for his music. Witness the pride and passion in his treatment of "Sunrise, Sunset", one of the numbers from the musical "Fiddler On The Roof".

In 2003, I was a member of a local amateur group, Waterloo and Crosby Theatre Company, and took part in the chorus of "Fiddler On The Roof" and I must admit the powerful expression of the music really made the hairs bristle on your neck.

As with all musical artistes, Frank had many strong influences on his singing career but the most obvious most certainly would have been the legendary Al Jolson.

Al Jolson, very sadly, died in 1950 at the age of 64 years just as Frankie was about to start making a name for himself in British showbusiness.

Jolson is acknowledged as one of the all time greats and founding fathers in the world of entertainment. The rich texture of his vocal fortissimo and the showy flamboyance of his hugely energetic stage performances inspired, indeed enthralled, artistes and audiences everywhere making him not only a famous name in American Vaudeville (Variety) but also one of the biggest stars ever to hit Broadway.

Against this kind of background it is no small wonder that Frankie Vaughan set himself the highest standards and put everything he had into his chosen vocation. Almost without exception everybody who went to see him perform live at any one of his shows will testify at its conclusion that they felt as though they had been royally and wonderfully entertained. Frankie had a dedicated commitment to his public and always put his heart and soul into everything he did, sometimes even a lot more.

Basil Tait, musical director and very good friend of Frank, from Newquay in Cornwall, relates some of the dynamic moments he observed whilst accompanying Frank on his hectic work schedules.

"In the eight years that I was Musical Director for Frankie Vaughan, even when sometimes he may have had personal worries, or was not feeling well, or when we lesser mortals might have felt like taking it a bit easy, Frank never ever gave less than 100% of himself when on stage. This was most noticeable to me when we were in Las Vegas in 1960. We did three shows a night, seven days a week and the last show of the night was at 2.30 am.!

Not surprisingly, at that time of the morning a lot of people in the audience had had quite a bit to drink and were probably only there to see the topless dancing girls! But at these shows Frank was even more determined than ever to win the audience over. Most people's attitude, certainly mine, would be "let's get it over with and get to bed," but Frank was just the reverse and he always got a tremendous ovation at the end of the show.

In 1967 we did a Christmas Season at the Alhambra Theatre in Glasgow, a city renowned for having very critical audiences, but they adored Frank there and every seat in the theatre was booked for the entire run of the show before we got there, Frank was determined that he would not let anyone down, come what may.

For a couple of weeks of the run he was desperately ill with bronchial pneumonia and running a very high temperature. He lived in the hospital during the day but at about 7.00 pm. the doctor gave him an injection to revive him, and we took him to the theatre and struggled to dress him and get him on stage. The doctor stood in the wings watching the time saying, "If he doesn't come off soon, within a few minutes, he'll probably collapse." But somehow he always made it and the audience never knew there was anything wrong with him. He risked his life doing it and we begged him to take a couple of days off but he was insistent that he couldn't disappoint anyone who had bought tickets to see him.

On the last night at the end of the show when Frank was thanking the audience for being so wonderful they all sang "Will Ye No Come

Back Ag'in" - a very moving and memorable moment."

Margaret Sutton, Hall Green in Birmingham describes another occasion when Frankie needed some medical attention before going on stage.

"I used to run the Lita Roza fan club in the '50's and '60's and often came across Frankie Vaughan when we travelled up and down the country to see Lita. In particular I remember meeting Frankie, I think it was at the Gaumont Theatre in Worcester, when he and Lita shared top of the bill. She closed the first half and he did the second half.

When Frankie arrived at the theatre he didn't feel too well, some kind of chest infection. I was with Lita in her dressing room and she asked me to go and see how he was. I went to his dressing room and he was having his throat and chest massaged and needless to say, everybody was a little worried.

However, in true showbiz fashion, when the time came for him to go on stage he went on and gave a superb performance as though nothing had happened. A true star!

Frank had a magnetic stage performance and he was a lovely man. Such a gentleman and a brilliant showman. Did you know that he was an honorary member of Lita's fan club? Lita is 78 years old now, still living in London and I speak to her regularly on the phone."

Lita Roza was born in Liverpool in 1926, a couple of years before Frankie and was brought up in a similar sort of area not very far from where he lived although I don't think they knew each other at the time.

Lita's father, also called Frank, was an accomplished accordion player and so Lita was introduced to the world of music at a very early age. She attended her first panto at the age of six and she knew then that a career in showbusiness was what she wanted to do.

By the time Lita reached her teens, she was appearing regularly in pantomime and went onto appear in the chorus of "Black Velvet" with Ted Ray and Jill Manners.

Despite being injured in the leg by a German bomber raid on Liverpool during the Second World War, Lita persisted with her showbiz aspirations and eventually landed a job as a singer with the Harry Roy band and from that point on she became one of the best loved female singers in the country.

Mrs. Doris Johnson from Tingley in Yorkshire, describes the impact Frankie made on her when he sang an Al Jolson number in a pub near Leeds.

"I have a lot of happy memories of Frankie Vaughan. I first saw him perform at a pub called The Ringway in Horsforth. I should say he was in his late teens or early twenties probably still at University. He was on his knees singing the old Al Jolson favourite, "Mammy". I was hooked from the very start and saw him many times after that.

In December 1987 my husband and I went on holiday to Woolacombe. Imagine my delight when I learned that Frankie was staying in the same hotel and was the artiste for the week.

He freely mixed with the guests with his wife, Stella, and family. He played snooker and seemed to really enjoy himself. I said to him, "Do you know where I first heard you sing?" He replied, "No, but I bet you are going to tell me." So I did and we had a real chuckle about it.

I always found him a friendly fellow, no airs, no graces. He is certainly greatly missed."

Monica Laverty from Wallsend, North Tyneside, also found Frankie to have no airs and graces and on one occasion she was lucky enough to receive free tickets to one of his shows.

"Frankie Vaughan was and still is my all time favourite singer. I have loved his style and music for more years than I care to remember. My now grown up family still tease me about my taste in music.

My friend's neighbour in Whitley Bay had a daughter engaged to be married to Frankie's son and when he was appearing in Newcastle he would stay with them. They knew of my devotion to his music so for his next appearance they gave me two tickets and an invitation to meet him backstage before the show. Back then films were not allowed to be shown on Sundays so they became regular concert nights.

His show was held in the Odeon Cinema, Newcastle, which recently closed. It was about April 1980. The programme was headed

'Popular Entertainments presents "The Frankie Vaughan Show."'

I will never forget that evening. Although married with two children I was like a teenager again. He made us so very welcome with a handshake so very genuine and the time he gave to chat to us was wonderful. A real gentleman, no airs and graces at all.

However, halfway through his show, when he announced his next song was for Monica I nearly collapsed with joy. The song was "Feelings", which is of course my favourite as it brings back memories of that special evening.

In 1994 Frankie did a season at the Cafe Royal, London. As I could not afford to go I sent him my good wishes and was informed it had been a great success. I was so very sad when he died and sent my condolences to Stella and family. She took the time to thank me in her own handwriting which showed that she was also a caring person. Obviously they were 'two of a kind.'

Frankie was not only a star, everyone knows how much he financially helped many organisations, especially for the youth, during his life."

However, it would seem that not every show that Frankie did went strictly according to plan as Vince Hunt from Gateshead, Tyne and Wear, reports,

"I saw Frankie Vaughan in the late sixties in Blackpool when the cordless microphone was still in its infancy. During his act he was playing hell with somebody off stage because his 'mike' wasn't right. I thought it a bit unprofessional and it is something that has always stuck with me. Funny how, after a show, you remember a thing like that and nothing else about it."

Frankie Vaughan always considered himself to be a very lucky person. He was grateful that fortune favoured him through the many traumas of his early life. His chance meeting with Stella who became his devoted wife and life-long friend. Having a lovely family of whom he could be justifiably proud. And, of course, being blessed with a wonderful talent which enabled him to make a living and a career out of one of his great passions in life – singing. Frankie loved to sing and entertain and make people happy anytime, anywhere, whether indoors or out in the open air, as Christine Lester from Ormesby in Middlesborough, found to her great joy one day.

"Frankie was a dear friend to me for many years, a very kind and caring man, especially as I haven't been too well for over 10 years. He went out of his way to boost me up, personal letters while I was in hospital, the best tonic anyone could ask for, and lots of daft, little things one example being one rainy golf day many years ago when he dived under my umbrella so he wouldn't get wet and we ended up walking along, both of us giggling and singing "We're Singing In The Rain."

Frankie made my life a lot more pleasant, kept me going while things were getting rough and through him I made lots of good friends who are always there for me.

One song he recorded was called "Think Beautiful Things", and quite often that's what Frank used to write at the end of his letters as he knew what the words of the song meant to me.

He is a sad loss to many friends and for many of us, having known such a special and wonderful person, life will never be the same again."

Frankie was also a source of great comfort and joy to Mrs. Audrey Amesbury of Caerphilly, Mid Glamorgan. He became her idol right from the first time she heard him sing "Green Door" all those many years ago and it became her life's ambition to meet him. "Quite simply he is Mr. Showbusiness," she said "and not only is he a wonderful performer but he has got a kind heart and does a lot for charity."

In October 1978 when Audrey found out that Frank was playing her local town at the Double Diamond Club it was a dream come true but because of many years of ill health and the fact that she was due to go into hospital on the very day that Frankie was doing his show, which was a Friday, she didn't quite know what to do. "There must be a way", she thought and in the end she pleaded with her doctors to admit her to hospital on the following Monday and let her attend the show to which they eventually agreed.

When Audrey's local newspaper "The News" heard this they contacted the management of the Double Diamond Club and a very special night was organised for her. Audrey and her husband, Basil, were met at the door of the club and escorted to the front seats. When Frank came on stage she was so excited but when he told the audience all about her and invited her on stage to present her with a bouquet of flowers, she just couldn't believe what was happening to her.

"After the show I was taken to Frankie's dressing room where he popped a bottle of champagne. He was fantastic and told me not to worry about going into hospital. I was more thrilled than ever with Frankie and I'll treasure that wonderful evening for the rest of my life. I cannot thank "The News" or the staff of the Double Diamond Club enough."

When Audrey went into hospital the following Monday she received further bad news.

"I was really devastated. Frank sent me a get well card and the words of his latest release "Think Beautiful Things" seemed to fit the way I was feeling. He wrote me again in January 1979 wishing me well.

He was a wonderful man, such a caring man. When he returned to the Double Diamond Club the next year I was able to go to the show and after he sang a few songs on stage he said, "There is a lady here tonight who I met last October and she was very ill. She is here tonight and thank God she is better."

Mrs. Irene Brayshaw from Chipping Sodbury in Bristol recalls the time Frankie gave an impromptu performance after the show.

"I worshipped Frankie Vaughan and a few years ago we were on holiday in Blackpool and our daughter and myself went to see Frankie on the North Pier. The show was fantastic and it was the last time I saw Frankie.

At the end of the show it was announced that Frankie would sign programmes in the foyer. I didn't need telling twice – whoosh I was gone!

The foyer became full, I was about seventh. He asked each person their name so that he could include it with his signature. When I said my name was Irene. He stopped what he was doing, stood up and sang "Goodnight Irene" all the way through. At the end everyone applauded.

It made my holiday that more special. I will always remember him. I am 78 now."

Jilly Cantwell of Acocks Green in Birmingham tells us of her impromptu claim to fame.

"In 1961 I was 16 years of age and worked in the typing pool of Birmingham Head Post Office and as quite a few of us were "Frankie Vaughan" mad (me, most of all) our Superintendent of Typists (we were civil servants in those days) allowed us to arrange a trip to see him in a show. I can't actually remember now whether we went to the Alexander Theatre or the Birmingham Hippodrome, probably the Hippodrome, but anyway we duly turned up and took our seats. These were front row, middle of the balcony and I was allowed the aisle seat because it was thought that being the smallest and the youngest I would want to 'jig about a bit.'

Frankie gave his usual polished performance, high kicks, dazzling smile, immaculately dressed and his ubiquitous cane and top hat. He drew the show towards the finale with the usual screaming and thunderous applause and, as the clapping died away, in that split second moment of total hush, I shot up from my seat and shouted at the top of my voice, "You haven't done "Green Door". There was a collective intake of breath and the full spot light was on me. The audience then began laughing and cheering and chanting "Green Door, Green Door."

Eventually he quietened us all down and said laughing, "And what is your name, my dear?" Blushing to my navel I replied, "Er ... Jilly." "Well, er Jilly," he said, "this is just for you." With that he went into the song "Green Door" keeping his eyes on me the whole time and blew me a kiss at the end. Of course he brought the house down and the audience wouldn't let him get off the stage.

I was 16 years old, 4'10" tall and oh-so -very innocent but I felt 10 foot after that. When I got home I proudly related all this to my mum but she wasn't as 'over the moon' as I thought she would be. C'est la vie."

However, it was not always the fans who had a lot to thank Frankie for, many stars did too, including fellow Liverpudlian, Miss Cilla Back as witnessed by L. Towers of Lancashire.

"In 1964 my daughter was age 12 and I took her to London to relatives for a holiday. At that time the Beatles were to the fore and Cilla

Black was just getting started in showbusiness.

We booked for a matinee show on the Monday afternoon at the London Palladium but I think the stage wasn't set up as good as it should have been because when Cilla came out onto the stage and started to sing you could hardly hear her.

The London Palladium is quite a large theatre and unfortunately people got restless and started to boo. Before it got too bad Frankie Vaughan must have realised what was happening and he swiftly came out on stage and started to sing along with her. The applause was tremendous.

Cilla must have been very grateful for what he did that day. He was a great performer and we thoroughly enjoyed the show – what a memory!"

Frankie Vaughan made a countless number of records during his recording career which spanned 1950 until 1968. Apart from 1966 he had hits every year from 1954 up to 1968.

His first recording in 1950 was on the Decca label, "The Old Piano Roll Blues", coupled with

"You're Daddy's Little Girl," why it wasn't a hit I'll never know, followed by his rendition of "Stay With The Happy People." Neither did very well and that was the end of the line as far as Decca was concerned.

From 1953 to 1955 he recorded 13 singles with HMV, his first one being "My Sweetie Went Away", but it was not until his sixth release that he made his first hit with a number entitled "Istanbul."

Frank's fortunes changed for the better when he signed for the newly formed Philips Recording Company with whom he stayed for a period of 11 years. His first with them was none other than "Give Me The Moonlight," which at Frankie's insistence, was on the 'B' side of "Tweedle Dee." "Give Me The Moonlight' of course was re-released in 1959 with "Happy Go Lucky" on the flip side, the total sales for "Give Me The Moonlight," exceeding one million copies.

In the mid 1950's, Lonnie Donegan started to dominate the British record charts with his short lived, individual brand of 'skiffle' music, quickly followed by the gigantic explosion of rock 'n' roll reverberating on both sides of the Atlantic, spearheaded by the likes of Elvis

Presley, Jerry Lee Lewis, Little Richard and Chuck Berry, but still Frankie held on in there. Although not rock 'n' roll himself, Frank did make some uptempo numbers such as "These Dangerous Years" in 1957 and "Loop De Loop" in 1963. It is said that when Ella Fitzgerald appeared at the London Palladium in 1963, she heard "Loop de Loop" and quite fancied doing it as part of her act but, unbeknownst to her, when she was halfway through the song, Frank walked onto the stage and finished it off with her, much to the tremendous delight and applause of the rapturous audience.

In 1956 Frank had his first top ten hit with "Green Door" which incidentally, was the 'B' side to "Pity The Poor Man". However, it was actually "Green Door" which reached the number two slot in the charts, being just pipped at the post by Johnny Ray's "Just Walking In The Rain."

1957 was probably Frankie's most prolific year as far as his records were concerned. He had a number one with "Garden of Eden", which also sold over a million and displaced Guy Mitchell's "Singing The Blues" at the top of the hit parade. Other hits in the same year included "These Dangerous Years," "Man On Fire", "You've Gotta Have Something In The Bank, Frank," "Kisses Sweeter Than Wine" and "Wandering Eyes."

In 1958 Frankie entered the American charts with a song called "Judy" and 1961 saw his version of "Tower of Strength" knock Elvis Presley's "His Latest Flame" off the very top of the U.K. charts.

With the demise of the rock 'n' roll originals in the early 1960's, nothing very special was happening on the music landscape until along came a guy named Chubby Checker with a new dance craze called "The Twist" and his recording of "Let's Twist Again" seemed to be forever on the airwaves.

In 1962 Frank was driving from Manchester to Leeds one stormy evening listening to his car radio and he got so taken with all this 'Twist' music that by the time he'd reached his destination he'd made his own contribution to this new musical phenomenon by writing his own "Don't Stop Twist" which ended up in the charts for a period of seven weeks.

When "The Twist" eventually petered out the market again went very quiet but then four uncontainable 'Mop Tops' from Liverpool collectively known as 'The Beatles' burst on the scene and turned the world of music unceremoniously onto its head, putting many of the old style crooners out of business.

In 1964 Frankie made his last record with Philips which was "Cabaret" from the hit musical of the same name.

One of my favourite Frankie Vaughan songs was "There Must Be A Way" which came out in 1967. I remember early 1968 when I was stationed at RAF Ballykelly in Northern Ireland and a few of us went to Quigley's Bar in the city of Londonderry for an evening out.

The Quigley Brothers had been one of the most successful Irish showbands for many years and naturally the atmosphere was alive with the best in musical entertainment.

During the course of the evening the very talented trio of keyboard, guitar and drums invited members of the audience to get up and give a song which I was persuaded so to do. For my party piece I chose "There Must be A Way" but the prestigious backing made such a mess of it, intentional or otherwise, that I vowed I would never attempt to do it again that is, until 2002, when I plucked up courage enough to give it another go, this time at Miss Patricia's Music Hall in Blackpool and it was a creditable success, largely due I might add, to the 'user friendliness' and craftsmanship of the highly accomplished keyboard player.

In the 1970's Frank concentrated more on what he liked doing best – live cabaret and concert work. He continued with his hectic work schedules appearing at all kinds of venues all over the country and further afield, including umpteen successive seasons at London's famous "Talk Of The Town".

There's the story that one evening towards the end of his show at the "Talk Of The Town", Jimmy Tarbuck came to the restaurant after appearing at the London Palladium in order to give Frank a lift home. By this time of course, Jimmy Tarbuck had changed out of his stage clothes and was now in 'scruff order' waiting in the wings for Frank to finish his act.

When Frankie spotted Jimmy Tarbuck he mischievously called Jimmy onto the stage but because he wasn't dressed for the part, he wasn't very keen to do so. However, after some gentle persuasion from Frank, he eventually came out and Frank, giggling, walked off the stage and left him to it, presumably thinking that he would go into a comedy routine. But, No! Jimmy Tarbuck turned the tables on Frank and went straight into "Hello Dolly". Frank came hurrying back on stage protesting that he hadn't yet done that song and both of them hilariously finished it off together much to the great amusement and delight of the audience.

Stan Livingston from the Lancashire market town of Ormskirk recalls when he saw Frank at one of Liverpool's popular night spots.

"I was always a great fan of this truly wonderful gentleman, Frankie Vaughan, and I had the privilege of meeting him only once throughout all the years.

I bought most of my suits from Denis Newton a much respected Liverpool tailor and I discovered he made suits for several showbiz clients, including Frankie. Denis would tell me of the times he'd either been out to dinner, attended a couple of showbiz functions or visited Frank at home with his family.

A few years ago a friend of mine, George Gregory, opened the "Scottie Club" in Great

Homer Street, Liverpool, as a cabaret venue, which later changed its name to the "Rendez Vous Club." I saw many acts there including Duncan 'Chase Me' Norvelle, Les Dennis and Dustin Gee, PJ Proby and many more. Knowing I was a fan of his, George phoned me to let me know he'd booked Frankie Vaughan and assured me he'd reserve me a couple of tickets for the night – there was no way I was going to miss it! This was 21 October 1983.

I've seen every film Frankie made and one of my big favourites had been "These Dangerous Years" and at the time the film was out you'd often hear me singing the song of the same name and doing the Frankie kick to accentuate every verse!

Anyway, after being superbly entertained by the great man in the "Rendez Vous Club" and having the advantage of some Dutch courage supplied by a generous intake of alcohol, I took the opportunity to approach him as he sipped a glass of wine with George and a few friends and fans at the bar. Within seconds I'd launched into:-

"Believe you me they're in a rut
Can't stand the way our hair is cut
They fix the blame on nothing but

These Dangerous Years
What do they know, what do they know
They never hear a voice inside them
crying
       "Go, go, go man go."

The "Go, go, go man go" bit was accompanied by the 'Frankie Kick' and was met with great approval by the man himself who certainly enjoyed the event and seemed delighted to hear someone repeating the song word perfect.

We all had a good laugh later. He was a really 'regular guy' and a superb gentleman who will always have my greatest respect.

The loss to showbiz is immeasurable. He's still greatly missed in a world that's fast becoming short of people who have talent, quality and calibre. He unselfishly gave back much to people who were not as fortunate as himself and I will always feel honoured to have met him even though it was only that once."

In 1985 Frank's career entered a new phase when he was chosen for the lead role in the musical "42nd Street" playing the part of Julian Marsh who was producing a new show entitled "Pretty Lady". For that reason "42nd Street" became known as the 'Show about a Show'.

The first performance took place at the New York Winter Gardens Theatre on 25 August 1980 and opened at the Theatre Royal in Drury Lane, London, on 8 August 1984 running for a total of 1,823 performances with James Laurenson as the original lead, Frank taking over some months later.

The story is that Julian Marsh has been badly hurt by the Wall Street Crash and needs to put on a successful show in order to recover some of his finances. As a result, he arranges for an ageing star, Dorothy Brock, to take the lead role in "Pretty Lady" knowing that her sugar daddy, Abner Dillon, would put up the money although Abner is not aware that Dorothy has a secret lover named, Pat.

In actual fact, a young hopeful, Peggy Sawyer, would have been better in the lead role in "Pretty Lady" but, for whatever reason, fails the audition and has to be content with just being an 'extra'.

Once rehearsals have been completed, an out of town show is put on prior to taking it to

New York but during the performance Peggy accidentally knocks Dorothy over who unfortunately breaks her ankle. Dorothy cannot continue and Peggy is so upset that she walks out of the show.

Julian Marsh is faced with a mega crisis. He pleads with Peggy to return to the show and take on the lead role but she is reluctant to do so and with only 36 hours to go before the show is due to open in New York, Julian eventually succeeds in persuading her to return.

After pushing her to the limits over such a short space of time the show is thankfully ready to go ahead and, against all the odds, is a huge success.

The part fitted Frankie to a 'T', but unfortunately after 12 months of pulling in the crowds, he had to pull out of the show due to ill health. This mishap seemed to signal a turning point in his career when one thing after another over the years to follow, would cause him to slow down and reduce considerably his professional workload.

In due course, sadly, very sadly, Frank's continuing health problems got the better of him and his very last public performance was at the Lord Grade Memorial Concert at the Prince of Wales in London. He sang a traditional, emotional lullaby accompanied by a lone violinist entitled "Rozinkes Mit Mandlen", translated, "Raisins and Almonds", the English words of which are written below and in some ways, proved to be quite prophetic.

"In the room of the temple In a cosy corner
There sits a widow all alone.
With her only little child she rocks gently
While singing a lovely lullaby.
And beneath the cradle
There's a little pure white goat
The little goat went out looking
Just as you'll do some day
Bringing raisins and almonds
      "Sleep, sweet baby, sleep."

Even in the days before his death, Frank was determined to the very end. He told the medical staff who were looking after him at the John Radcliffe Hospital, in Oxford, "I would just like to do one more show to raise funds for the hospital."

Frankie Vaughan, indeed, a truly remarkable man.

Frank with Marilyn Monroe

Frank with Mrs. Doris Johnson

Frank with Audrey Amesbury

Frank at the Rendez Vous Club, Liverpool

Frank at the Rendez Vous Club, Liverpool

The "Good Old Days"

Southport Theatre Programme

Frankie Vaughan

Keith O'Keefe
Dumarte and Denzer
Dolly Set

Plus

ROY HILTON & HIS ORCHESTRA
Drummer for Frankie Vaughan - KEN HEBDEN

Executive Producer — DANNY SILVER

FOR SOUTHPORT THEATRE

STAGED BY	ROSALYN WILDER
COMPANY MANAGER	MIKE CARMICHAEL
CHOREOGRAPHER	MELODY URQUHART-ATTIAS
DIRECTOR OF TOURISM AND ATTRACTIONS	PHIL KING
COMPLEX MANAGER AND LICENSEE	STEVE FARROW
ASSISTANT MANAGER	IAN ROGERS
HOUSE ENGINEER	DON SYKES
STAGE MANAGER	PATRICK BOWES

Southport Theatre programme

FRANKIE VAUGHAN

c/o *Clifford Elson
(Publicity) Ltd.
15, Oxford Circus Ave.,
231, Oxford Street, W.1.*

21st January, 1979.

Mrs. A. Amesbury,

My dear Audrey,

How nice to hear from you and to receive the cuttings; it was a pleasure for me to meet you and I am delighted to know that THINK BEAUTIFUL THINGS was such a help to you after the operation. I hope it was a great success and that you are now reaping the benefit and feeling much better.

Let's hope we meet up again one of these days but meantime I would like to wish you and yours good health and every happiness in '79.

Fondest regards.

Frank

FRANKIE VAUGHAN

c/o Alan Field (Promotions) Ltd.,
11 Arden Road,
Finchley
London N3 3PB

24th February 1983

Mrs. Audrey Amesbury

Dear Audrey,

Thank you so much for your lovely letter — how nice to
hear from you.

I have signed the lovely photograph which was taken when
we met at the Club Double Diamond and hope that it won't
be too long before we have the opportunity of meeting
again. I would love to appear in your area again — I am
just waiting to be asked!

My fondest regards to you and yours,

Sincerely,

Frankie Vaughan

3.

FRANKIE VAUGHAN

A
Life Celebré

Frankie Vaughan was born Frank Ephraim Abelson on 3 February, 1928 and was brought up in number 39 Devon Street in the Islington area of Liverpool by his father, Isaac, mother, Leah, and his Russian born grandmother, along with his three younger sisters, Myra, Phyllis and baby Carol.

Frankie's middle name, Ephraim, is the same as that given to the second son of Joseph who traces his line back to Abraham, father of the Jewish people. Ephraim was responsible for an important tribe in the Northern Kingdom of Israel, often referred to by his name. Quite apt for Frank really in view of the great

107

respect and recognition he was to earn for himself later on in life.

12 Months after Frank was born saw the beginnings of a world recession which went on for at least another four years. In actual fact the 1930's were troubled times for just about everybody everywhere from social as well as political perspectives. There was continual Communist agitation, widespread industrial unrest, the growth of Fascism both here and in Europe and the ominous rumblings of impending world war. Add to that high unemployment, large scale 'means testing', hunger marches all over the country and the ever present threat of the dreaded workhouses and you don't have the most salutary conditions for a young child to grow up in.

Devon Street was very close to London Road which led down to Liverpool's famous Empire Theatre. Little did Frank know that one day he would play top billing at that most luxurious venue.

Eddie Hope from Fairfield in Liverpool remembers the time he met Frankie when he was playing there in the Christmas panto in 1960. At the end of the show, Eddie, being a great fan of Frankie, went round to the stage door to get his autograph. He produced an old photograph of Frankie in his army uniform which had been taken whilst he was serving in Aden during his National Service days in the Middle East. Eddie continues:

"Frankie took one look at the photo and burst out laughing. "Where did you get this?" he asked, absolutely amazed. Jimmy Tarbuck was nearby and Frank called him over to show him the photo. The two of them were laughing their heads off and rather than just stand there, I joined in laughing with them.

Frank was a very pleasant and most sincere man."

Even littler did Frank know that on the 25 September 1998 he would formally open the prestigious Crowne Plaza Hotel on Liverpool's waterfront on the very same spot where he proposed to his wife, Stella, all those years ago, during their courtship days, whilst he was showing her the different places he used to frequent as a Liverpool youngster in the 1930's.

My grandfather, James Beck Finn, came from Lancaster down to Liverpool in 1907 and in the 1930's he had a coal yard in Langsdale Street, only minutes away from Devon Street, where Frankie lived. He used to carry the coal, travelling around the neighbourhood to his customers, by sturdy horse and cart, and almost certainly, would have provided Frank and his family with their weekly delivery of coal.

Funnily enough, when Frank was evacuated to Lancaster during the Second World War, he lived at the address, 25 Moor Lane, which was only minutes away from where my grandfather had lived in Lancaster, at number 40 Long Marsh Lane.

The Islington area of Liverpool, a tough neighbourhood on the edge of the City centre, was very grimy and smoky and of narrow, poorly lit streets lined on both sides with old, decaying and overcrowded terraced houses, cramped as well as damp. Not the most healthy of places in which to live and where many of its inhabitants would suffer from a multiple variety of bronchial ailments. The majority of the population was immigrant, mainly of Irish origin, many of whom lived, indeed existed, in dreadfully appalling and squalid conditions.

Against this kind of background it is no wonder that some members of such a community would grow up resentful of authority and adopt anti social and aggressive attitudes. Yet many others would pull themselves up by their boot straps and resolve to do something positive and creative with their lives. The grit and determination of Frank Abelson would unquestionably have energised him towards the latter.

In the 1950's I went to the Liverpool Collegiate, an elitist grammar school, in Shaw Street just across the road from Devon Street. Most incongruous really, having a finely architectured edifice of style and grandeur placed right in the heart of a poverty area. We would walk to school from all different angles wearing our neat, black blazers, short trousers and school caps carrying leather satchels over our shoulders whilst some of the locals walked on the other side of the road quite literally dressed in rags, holes in their shoes and eating jam butties on their way to school, sometimes with the jam smeared along the sides of their faces. On occasions we would be attacked by stone throwing gangs.

Because there wasn't a lot of money around in the 1930's, both of Frank's parents had to go out to work in order to make ends meet. His father, Isaac, was an upholsterer, and his mother, Leah, a seamstress, trades for which then there would have been a big demand in the local area. As a result they both worked long and hard from early morning till late at night and Frank and his younger sisters were left in the charge and capable hands of their Russian born grandmother. Being a very young lad at the time Frank, of course, would have considered himself to be the man of the house and naturally very protective towards the all female household. Although inherently a gentle and caring person, to survive on the streets of a densely populated city, Frank had to be able to look after himself and evidence of his attributes in this particular arena has been borne out by his boxing skills both at Lancaster Lads Club and during his days in the British army.

I remember some years ago I saw Frank on a television chat show, I think it was one of the David Frost shows, and at the time, because of a high profile case involving a householder thumping a burglar, the current topic of public debate was how far can one legally go to restrain a burglar pending the arrival of the police.

The host put a scenario to Frankie and asked him what he would do if he was confronted by a burglar at home who was threatening his family. Without pausing one moment Frank firmly replied, "I'd wring his bloody neck!"

It is apparent that Frank's grandmother had a great influence on him during his formative years and instilled in him the importance and value of strong family ties, a lesson which he carried personally and admirably throughout his entire life.

Originally, Liverpool was just a small fishing village with salmon swimming up and down the River Mersey and it is hard to believe that not so long back in 1558, its population only amounted to around a thousand people. However, all that was to change as the port of Liverpool began to grow in stature.

In the 19th century, countless numbers of people from all four corners of the world descended upon Liverpool looking for ships to take them to a better way of life in the New World. Many were Jewish people fleeing from extreme religious persecution in Russia and other European countries whose numbers by 1914 had reached 11,000, not forgetting of course, the multitudes of Irish people escaping from the ravages of the Potato Famine in 1840's.

It often happened that when immigrants arrived in Liverpool after trekking over long distances for long periods of time, they found they didn't have enough money left to buy a voyage to the Americas, or whilst waiting ages for the long, drawn out passages to take place, many would decide to stay and put down their family roots where they stood.

Fortunately for Liverpool in many respects, a lot of colour, character, culture and creativity was injected into the development of the city as it entered the 20th century.

As soon as the young Abelson started his schooling in Liverpool his artistic talents were quickly recognised by his teacher. She was so impressed with the representation of his drawings, particularly those of his animals, that she asked his mother to come up to the school to see her.

Initially, Leah thought Frank had been up to some kind of mischief but when she saw the quality of his work for herself, she too was so excited she couldn't wait to get home and tell her husband. Isaac was not exactly ecstatic about it, he had plans for Frank to take up a trade and to follow in his father's footsteps as an upholsterer or perhaps become a cabinet maker, but there was no way he was going to stand in the way of his son's natural abilities.

Frank attended the long established Liverpool Hebrew School located at the junction of Hope Place and Pilgrim Street which is now an annexe of Liverpool John Moores University and alongside the popular Unity Theatre. He received a traditional Jewish education which was to stay with him throughout his entire life. This, together with his singing in the Princes Road Synagogue choir, formed the solid foundations on which he was able to build his later illustrious future.

Leslie Cantor, retired Liverpool businessman, went to Liverpool Hebrew School around the same time as Frankie and remembers seeing him on several occasions. Asked of his thoughts regarding Frank, Les replied with feeling, "Just an ordinary guy; just an ordinary guy," a sentiment echoed by none other than one of Britain's topmost entertainers, Bruce

Forsyth, some 60 years later when asked for his comments following Frank's death in 1999.

Alas, the dark clouds of World War Two began to gather and rumbled ominously across the lands and horizons of continental Europe. It was the start of many years of disruption to Frank Abelson's upbringing.

In 1939 Britain declared war on Nazi Germany, a war which would affect every man, woman and child, indeed the whole of mankind. With Liverpool considered the second city of England and a major seaport vital for the supply route between Britain, the USA and Canada, it was feared that Liverpool and its environs would become a prime target for the bombs of the ruthless German Luftwaffe. In addition to that, there were intelligence reports of a possible poison gas attack and immediate arrangements were made to evacuate all the children and other vulnerable persons to safer parts of the country. As a result, the government required all relevant local authorities to appoint a Billeting Officer for the purpose of receiving and accommodating such people.

During the first week of September 1939, over 50,000 school children and 34,000 mothers with under school age children left the Liverpool area to seek refuge in towns and villages across the North West and beyond.

On 1 September 257 children from Liverpool Hebrew School including Frank Abelson, boarded a train at Liverpool's Central Station and set off for the the City of Chester where they were met and billeted at several houses in various areas of the Cheshire town. For many it was not only their first time away from their home but also their first time away from their mothers and much shedding of tears took place.

The weeks passed by but nothing happened. There were no signs of any fighting or hostilities and this period came to be known as 'The Phoney War'. As a result, by January 1940, large numbers of children had eagerly returned to their homes and families in Liverpool.

However, this time of peace and calm was not to last. In August 1940 the bombing began. And how! By the end of April 1941 there had been no less than 60 German air raids, any of which could last from as little as a few minutes or as long as an eternity of 10 hours involving anything from a few to as many as 300 aircraft. 2000 People were killed and thousands more badly injured. But worse was yet to come.

The savage ferocity of the brutal and continual bombardment of buildings, churches, houses and the docks during the first week of May 1941 went down in the annals of history as the infamous May Blitz, with Liverpool suffering the largest number of civilian casualties of any British city outside London.

870 tonnes of bombs and 112,000 incendiary devices were mercilessly and indiscriminately dropped on Liverpool and its surrounding areas. Nearly 2000 people were killed, well over 1000 injured and 65,000 homes variously damaged making thousands of people destitute and homeless.

But the resolve of the Liverpool people was aptly summed up by the defiant words of the indomitable Mrs. Dorothy Laycock, "They tried to wipe us of the face of the earth but didn't quite, did they?" Even Winston Churchill, Britain's war time Prime Minister, was moved to remark, "I see the damage done by the enemy attacks but I also see the spirit of an unconquered people."

Faced by such extreme dangers, the children of Liverpool 'upped sticks' once again and moved on to other and safer places in the country but this time not to Chester. Frank and his two younger sisters, Myra and Phyllis, were evacuated to the tiny Westmoreland, as it was then, village of Endmoor where they were put up at the home of the kindly, Mr and Mrs Stan Johnson. The rest of the family remained in Liverpool.

Endmoor, now Cumbria, is located on the A65 road midway between Kendal and Kirby Lonsdale and during the 1939-45 war it was home to lots of evacuees from the Liverpool and Newcastle areas. Frank and his two sisters must have been bewildered by the beautiful scenery and lush green fields of this quiet, tranquil environment after experiencing the chaos and mess of wartime Liverpool.

However, even though Endmoor was well off the beaten track, the hearts and minds of the local people were not completely untouched by a war that was raging round the world on many fronts.

The children of the village did their bit by picking rose hips for the making of syrup and nettles for medicinal purposes. They also spent many hours picking the leaves and the grass out of the heaps of sphagnum moss which, because of its antiseptic properties, was widely used in the dressings of servicemen's wounds. Summerlands House, a large Victorian mansion at the north end of Endmoor, also, served as a rest and rehabilitation centre for sick and injured seamen of the Merchant and Fishing fleets.

As the war got progressively worse, the demand for more soldiers grew beyond all expectations so that older men had to be conscripted to serve in the armed forces. Frank's father, Isaac, was called up into the army with the result that Frank's grandmother and mother, Leah, with Carol, decided to move to Lancaster where they were joined by Frank, Myra and Phyllis who came down from Endmoor which was only 15 miles away. The whole family, with the exception of Isaac, was all together again.

Although the general way of life in Lancaster, originally called Lun Castrum – the fort on the River Lune, was a big improvement on that in

Liverpool, living conditions still left a lot to be desired.

In the 1930's a lot of the population lived in closely packed terraced houses tucked into narrow, cobbled alleys. The best could be described as clean, whitewashed and brightened up with fresh flowers but the worst were often dark, miserable and damp and easy prey for the spread of infectious disease. Drinking water was sourced from communal wells and standpoints and earth closets provided the main means for shared toilet facilities.

During the war years, even though Lancaster was not on a regular flight path for German bombing raids, it was still very much the appearance of a busy garrison town. The Canadians were billeted at the King's Arms Hotel in Lancaster and also at the Grosvenor Hotel in Morecambe. The King's Own Royal Regiment was stationed in Lancaster and the RAF and WRAF in Morecambe. There were lots of shows and dances for the entertainment of the troops as well as the local population and for a young teenager of 14 years of age, this would have been Frank's first real taste of, and introduction to, the world of showbusiness.

Frank lived with his family at number 25 Moor Lane, off Great John Street, which was a terraced house with an outside privy. A privy could be little more than a hole in the ground with a single piece of wood to sit on or if you were really posh, a hole in the ground with a makeshift wooden seat.

It was in the garden of this house that Frank made his very first public appearance in a concert party organised by himself and a few of his friends in order to raise some funds for the poor people of the Faroes where his father was stationed in the army. They raised the princely sum of £14.

When 25 Moor Lane was demolished some years later, appropriately enough, the Duke's Playhouse now called the Duke's Theatre Cinema, was built there and when Frank was in the area with his wife, Stella, in 1982, they had the great pleasure of visiting the Duke's Playhouse and he described it as "absolutely fabulous".

Frank was not a person to let the grass grow under his feet and within days of moving to

Lancaster he was back behind a desk at the Boys National School intent on pursuing his artistic studies. At the age of 14 he won a scholarship to Lancaster College of Art and it seemed that this was the direction in which his future career was destined to go.

Whilst he was at the College he took the opportunity to give vent to one of his other talents, singing with the College dance band which played at various venues including hospitals, old peoples homes and the Storey's Institute. Mrs. Thelma Simpson of Morecambe remembers seeing Frank one evening at the Storey's Institute.

"When Frankie lived in Lancaster there used to be a dance at the Storey's Institute on Saturday nights (I think this was the Art School at the time) and they were called crazy nights because it was only half a penny (in old money) to go in. I did once go with friends from Morecambe and did actually dance with him but only for a short time as he was very popular, extremely good looking and also very friendly with everybody."

Frank's natural enthusiasms and energies also brought about his early gravitation towards Lancaster Lads Club which was responsible for creating a major turning point in his life, a fact to which he constantly referred and expressed gratitude for, throughout his entire life. He often said that his membership of Lancaster Lads Club kept him on the straight and narrow during his teenage years and helped set him up in life. Hence his unstinting determination to put back into the Boys' clubs movement what he got out although, in his case, what he put back was multiplied many times over.

When Frank walked through the doors of the Dallas Road club it was as if a whole new world of opportunity and enterprise had been opened up before his very eyes and it wasn't very long before he was taking advantage of all that was on offer – table tennis, snooker, football, swimming, even boxing, an odd choice really, considering his gentle manner and thought for other people. Later on in life though, Frank went in for much quieter and more relaxed activities such as playing golf and trout fishing. He would be at his most peaceful sitting comfortably on a river bank gently puffing at a cigar, waiting for a bite. He had many photographs at home of those that didn't get away.

Mary Braithwaite of Southport happened to meet Frank one day during one of his fishing moments.

"My late parents, Sidney and Charlotte Cheale, were Christian Evangelists helping children to understand the Bible and Christianity. Each year we had six weeks of camping for dozens of children.

One year the camps were in Barcombe Mills in Sussex. We camped by the woods and a beautiful river called the Ouse. I was about eight years old and my friends called me one day to see Frankie Vaughan who was fishing by the waterfall.

The waterfall was by a beautiful bridge and salmon were trying to jump up the waterfall. Frankie must have known of this beautiful secret place as he was having a fishing holiday.

He was just as lovely and smiling as on the television and I also remember his beautiful speaking voice that sounded like the lovely waterfall. He was very successful in catching some of the salmon."

Frank also had a keen interest in horse racing. Douglas Marks writes from Marlborough in Wiltshire:

"As a fan and horse trainer, I asked Frank to let me train for him. Our first horse was named 'The Jazz Singer' but he was so slow in one race the stewards had the jockey in for not trying. He had other more successful horses including 'Razmataz' and 'Asa Yolson' and we were partners in breeding the odd winner.

He was a lovely guy with a lovely wife. I used to enjoy his singing - still do. Although I was just a fan he let me get to know him as a mate. Who could ask for more?"

Martin Langsdale, West Bridgford, Notts, remembers seeing Frank at a race meeting.

"Back in the 1970's when I did a casual job at Nottingham racecourse. I remember spotting a group of well dressed and tanned men. On returning to my place in the stands my thoughts were confirmed when I heard people saying, "It's Frankie Vaughan."

Among the group was a man similar looking to Frankie. Could it have been his brother?"

Afraid not, Martin, Frank had no brothers. Just three sisters. Quite possibly his cousin.

The National Association of Boys Clubs, now called, in the interest of political correctness, the National Association of Clubs for Young People, was a charity very close to Frank's heart. The amount of time he devoted to the movement is already legend. Raising funds for them was something he never tired of.

It was as if he thought he could never repay the indebtedness he felt he owed for the lasting impact the years he spent at Lancaster Lads Club had had on a future he could only ever have dreamed about.

Not only did he donate the royalties from many of his records including such hits as 'Green Door' and 'You've Got To Have Something In The Bank, Frank' but also regularly subscribed the proceeds from one week of his working year to their funds. In 1955 he helped raise a total of £20,000 and by 1970 the spectacular sum of £1 million had been achieved. But it didn't end there. In 1971 he continued in the same vein. In one week he did a show in Morecambe to benefit Lancashire Association of Boys Clubs followed by another at Ewell in Surrey for the Surrey

A.B.C., went on to Dunstable a few days later to raise money for the Buckinghamshire Boys Club and then finished off at the Piccadilly in London for the Boys' Clubs in Essex. And if that wasn't enough, whenever he could, he would actually visit the clubs and sign autographs in exchange for a donation or give a performance free of charge. In 1955 he did a show at Sedbergh Boys Club in Bradford and Mrs. C. Davies of Cardiff, who was a concert party artiste herself as a teenager, remembers working with Frank at the Central Boys Club on the corner of Bute Street in her own home town.

In 1958 at the Gaumont Cinema in Worcester, his autograph hunters were charged a fee in order to swell the coffers of the NABC and at a jumble sale in the Carnegie Boys Club, Moseley, he sold his autographs for the proud sum of one shilling (five pence).

In October 1981, Frank had the great pleasure of re-visiting Lancaster Lads Club in order to open the new and magnificent all weather sports arena, visible evidence of all those years of hard work and the efforts he had invested so selflessly, even during times when he was at the height of his fame.

Towards the end of the war, Frank's father, Isaac, was invalided out of the Army and rather than return to Liverpool and start all over again he decided to settle in Leeds to be near his brother who had established a timber business there. For Frank and the rest of the family, it was a case of here we go again.

The tenacious Frank lost no time in getting himself into Leeds College of Art. Exams were fast approaching and he was keen not to let the opportunity of gaining a professional qualification pass him by. In any case, military service was looming large on the horizon and he wanted to make sure the academic phase of his life was well and truly behind him before concentrating his mind on serving King and Country.

Frank entered the Royal Army Medical Corps and hence would be considered as a non-combatant. A large part of his service was spent in the Middle East, in Malta and Egypt. During his off duty hours he kept his vocal chords in good shape by singing in local clubs and at Army concerts when the occasions arose. He also took advantage of the many sporting facilities on offer which included the opportunity for him to sharpen up on his previously acquired boxing skills. Rather strange really for somebody who was effectively classed as a non combatant.

In any event, either Frank didn't have that many fights or he was such an adept tactician, he was able to duck and dodge any blows that came his way, because his face bore none of those features usually associated with members of the boxing fraternity. Perhaps his opponents didn't want to spoil his good looks. However, one consolation of Frank being a medic was that if he did deliver a knock out blow to any of his adversaries he would at least have been able to administer first aid to them straight away.

While Frank was in the Army he was delighted to learn that he had successfully passed all his exams and was now the proud holder of an Arts degree.

On demob, Frank returned to his family in Leeds and started to undergo his teacher training. In view of his exam success it would appear that this was the obvious career path for him to take although deep down the urge to keep on singing as a second string to his bow was very much still on his mind.

Shortly after Frank's arrival in Leeds, his father, Isaac, who was a member of Leeds Royal British Legion asked the concert secretary of the club to give his son a trial spot for which Frank received the grand sum of thirty shillings (£1.50) but not a lot seemed to come of it.

It was whilst in Leeds that Frank had the good fortune to meet his wife to be. Stella was a friend of Frank's younger sister, Myra, and one night when they were at the Locarno Ballroom, Frank came walking in. Myra instinctively introduced Frank to Stella. It was love at first sight and a love, so strong and true, it was to last a lifetime. On 6 June 1951, Frank and Stella married and were subsequently blessed with three children, David, who was born in 1953, Susan in 1956 and Andrew, 1965. It was indeed a family of real outstanding virtue.

With Stella at his side Frank continued to flourish and after winning a local crooning competition he went on to appear at the famous City of Varieties. And there was more. Whilst performing at the Leeds Empire during a College Rag Revue, Frank was 'spotted' by the BBC radio producer, Barney Colehan, who gave him a letter of introduction to take to Billy Marsh, a highly regarded agent with the Delfont organisation, to use anytime he happened to be in London.

Around the same time it just so happened that Frank also entered and won a nationwide arts competition and he was invited to display his work at a furniture exhibition in London's Earls Court. On the back of this success, Frank decided to move with Stella to London and explore the possibility of carving out for himself a career as a commercial artist. But it wasn't that easy.

Desperate and not knowing which way to turn, Frank contacted Billy Marsh and produced the letter given him by Barney Colehan. He was given an audition and Billy Marsh was so impressed he booked Frank straight away to appear on the Jimmy Wheeler Show playing the Kingston Empire in Surrey. Amongst the numbers he did was "Powder Your Face With Sunshine" and he brought the house down. Frank was on the front page of the papers the following day hailed as the country's latest singing sensation.

Within weeks of playing the Kingston Empire Frank was hired to do a week long stint at the

Hulme Hippodrome in Manchester for a handsome fee of £100 which was a big jump from the £5 a week he had been getting as a commercial artist. Following on from that, Val Parnell booked him to do a tour of the vast Moss Empire circuit. He couldn't go wrong. One occasion he was on the same bill as the veteran entertainer, Issy Bonn, who remarked after the show, "Watch that lad, he's going to be big one of these days" and how right he was. Frank became such a big draw in the 1950's with many chart successes and a number of film roles that by the end of the decade he had crossed the Atlantic to wow them in the United States.

Frankie Vaughan was the first British artiste to make it mega in America paving the way in later years for others to follow suit including Tom Jones, Englebert Humperdink and, arguably, the Beatles with their re-branding of early rock'n'roll. The American establishment began to sit up and take notice that there was a rich seam of musical talent in this lovely, little island of ours.

Frank was warmly welcomed at the Copacabana in New York, receiving a rapturous standing ovation, and appeared on television in the Perry Como and Patti Page shows. He also had a spot on the annual Bob Hope World Wide Special elevating his reputation as a world class entertainer to newer and greater heights.

Frank went on to play the Dunes Hotel in Las Vegas and impressed the audience even more. At the end of his first show there was a huge, vociferous demand for him to do an encore for which he wasn't entirely prepared and so he finished off by singing "When I Fall In Love" accompanied only by his musical director, Ray Long, on the piano. The applause was so tremendous he decided to make it a regular feature of his act. His reviews met with such high acclaim that he was booked to return and do a full season.

However, his fans at home were getting really concerned. They thought Frank would get to like America so much that he would be tempted to stay there but he tried to assure them they had no need to worry and that he would soon return to the U.K. He considered that his experiences in the States not only would play a vital part in furthering his show business career and self development but also be instrumental in enhancing his professional status as a superstar on the international stage. But when Frank started to rub shoulders with the likes of Sammy Davis Junior, Elvis Presley and Bobby Darin, and, following a visit to the Beverley Hills home of Roger Moore and Dorothy Squires, there was talk of his embarking upon a Hollywood film career, many of his fans in Britain were becoming overwrought with anxiety especially when he was chosen to star opposite the world's most glamorous woman, Marilyn Monroe, in the movie "Let's Make Love."

Fortunately, the 'glam and glitt' of Hollywood didn't quite gel and he realised his family, and his friends and fans, back home were far more important to him than anything else. He returned to Britain mellowed yet triumphant in the knowledge that he had been there and given a good account of himself but the celluloid world of cinema was not the life for him.

Frank arrived in Britain completely unaffected by the fame of his Hollywood experience and was very soon back into a busy performance schedule doing what he did and liked best, playing to live audiences at cabaret venues up and down the country.

He regularly appeared at the prestigious 'Talk Of The Town' theatre restaurant and the famous 'London Palladium' and continued to pack them in at the clubs, theatres and hotels in all his favourite towns and seaside resorts. He also played many seasons at Blackpool's North Pier and in the family variety shows on television.

Even though Frank had turned his back on a Hollywood movie career he did make another film in Britain entitled "It's All Over Town" but it was described more as a pop extravaganza featuring Acker Bilk, the Bachelors, the Springfields and the Hollies, than a dramatic acting role.

And if that wasn't enough, he still found time to push ahead with his unrelenting fund raising efforts for the benefit of the Boys Clubs and other charities, reaching incredible, record levels of achievement by the end of the decade.

Margaret Westwood of Ormskirk in Lancashire recalls the occasion when Frank came to a boys' club near her.

"Around 1966/7 I worked at the time for the Walsall Education Department in one of the town's youth clubs. Frankie Vaughan as you know was very involved with the Boys' Clubs at the time and was invited by the Education Committee to re-open the Goscot Boys' Club after it had been completely refurbished.

Because I worked for the department I was lucky enough to be invited to attend the opening and went with my husband and daughter who at the time was eight years old and Frankie's most devoted fan.

It was a lovely, happy day. Frankie Vaughan was charming and pleasant to all, he smiled and waved to everyone and shook hands with many people there. He stayed to meet as many of the boys as he could before leaving.

Altogether a very happy day and good for the town to have a new club for the boys to go to."

In 1985, at 57 years of age Frank's career turned in a new direction. He was chosen for the lead in the hit musical, "42nd Street" at the Drury Lane Theatre in London's West End, playing the part of the ebullient Broadway producer, Julian Marsh, a very physical and energy sapping role.

After a hectic 12 months of treading the boards, Frank came out of the show. It was said that he injured his foot although other reports suggest there may have been some 'behind the scenes' acrimony.

Nevertheless, the end of this particular period in Frank's life seemed to mark the beginning of a number of health problems that were to dog him for the years to follow.

Shortly after his departure from Drury Lane, he was treated for peritonitis, an acute inflammation of the abdominal organs which can cause death if not quickly treated in hospital, and in the early 1990's, what was originally suspected to be a pulled muscle in his back, sustained during a game of golf, turned out to be the first of a worrying series of aneurysms.

An aneurysm is the local swelling of an artery just like a blow out on an inner tube which can get worse if it is weakened by the high blood pressure of a person who may be prone to that kind of condition.

The artery most usually affected is the aorta, the main artery of the chest and abdomen. The most serious risk posed by an aneurysm would be the possibility of a rupture between the inner and outer layers of the arterial wall, thus putting the life of the patient in extreme danger.

As if that wasn't enough to contend with, in the mid 1990's, Helen and Derek Pellatt of Ormskirk, Lancashire, happened to see Frankie in a wheelchair.

"In September 1995, Helen and myself went on a short week end cruise from Liverpool to Dublin on the 'Southern Cross' and Frankie Vaughan was to be the entertainer on the Saturday evening.

Following an enjoyable day in Dublin, as we were boarding the ship someone in a wheelchair was being assisted into a lift. We were not able to see who was in the wheelchair. However, it quickly went round the ship that the person in the wheelchair was Frankie Vaughan. Would he be able to perform that evening? At the evening performance all was revealed.

Frank came on stage using arm crutches for support. He explained to the audience that he had recently undergone operations on both of his knees but he was on his way to recovery.

Then he went into his act which lasted for well over an hour and he was excellent. What a man! What a performer! Absolutely superb."

That is total dedication. It demonstrates clearly the commitment and calibre of Frankie Vaughan. At the time he would have been 67 years of age and he could quite easily have called off the show. People would have understood perfectly. But, no, he wasn't one to let people down and this despite the fact that he was performing on board ship in waters that can get very rough to say the least.

Unfortunately, brighter days were not to appear. In May 1999, Frank was admitted to the John Radcliffe Hospital in Oxford where he underwent emergency heart surgery. A ruptured major blood vessel leading to his heart had started to leak and despite the superlative efforts of the medical staff, he was to remain in intensive care for the last year of his life.

Even so, eternal optimist and devoted professional that he was, Frank held on for as long as he could before cancelling any of the bookings he knew he wasn't going to be able to make, one of which included topping the bill in Radio Merseyside's show in the July at the famous Summer Pops bonanza in Liverpool's King's Dock. In the September he was due to play in a charity golf classic in Hoylake on the Wirral peninsular and on the 15th of the same month, to headline a show at Liverpool Empire, celebrating the 50th Anniversary of the Variety Club of Great Britain, but he was too ill and too weak to attend.

When I was a young teenager in the 1950's, I was in the 22nd Liverpool Company of the Boys' Brigade and just like Frankie, I considered that my membership of a youth organisation helped to keep me 'on the straight and narrow'.

However, when I left the Boys' Brigade in 1959, for many years after, I regularly attended the Annual Re-Union Dinners which were held in the centre of Liverpool. In 1971 I attended as usual and at the end of a scrumptious meal, the time arrived for the Company Captain, Mr. Ron Cross, to speak to the gathered assembly. He stood up and announced that due to the changing attitudes and lack of interest in traditional B.B. values by the up and coming generation, he had decided to call it a day and close down the Company. There was a collective gasp all around the room followed by a stunned silence. There was an air of disbelief as Mr. Cross continued with the rest of his address.

At the time I lived in Skelmersdale in Lancashire and after the Re-union I was driving home along a stretch of country road through the village of Melling when it suddenly hit me. The sudden shock of what Mr. Cross had said exploded right in front of me and my mind was engulfed in a sense of great loss. I felt that part of the institution of my growing up had been torn from within me. I pulled into the side of the road for a couple of minutes until I recovered enough to continue with the rest of my journey.

At 6pm. on Friday, 17 September 1999, I was driving along the very same stretch of road in Melling on my way to teach at St. Bede's Night School in Ormskirk when the news came over the car radio that Frankie Vaughan had died earlier that day and had been buried that same afternoon. I experienced exactly the same feelings as before. A sense of shock and a feeling of great loss. It was as if another part of my life had been cruelly taken away.

Indeed, for Frank's family and close friends, and for the many thousands of people not only in Britain but also across the Earth's oceans who mourned the sadness of his passing, the world, from that point on, became a much poorer place. The Lord Mayor of Liverpool, Councillor Joe Devaney, paid tribute to Frank, "He was a wonderful ambassador for the City and always remained loyal to Liverpool."

Forever remembered will be the name, Frankie Vaughan.

There are several versions as to how Frankie came by the name Vaughan albeit the vast majority are generally variations of a similar theme. Bill Manley of Llandaff in Cardiff, states,

"His nan was a Russian Jew and could only speak broken English. After Frank's birth when she held him for the first time, she said, "He is my first 'vorn' (born)" and that is why he took the stage name of Vaughan. I heard this on the radio some years ago. My wife and I thought he was absolutely great."

Mrs. Audrey Fox from Farnley in Leeds has another view.

"Frankie Vaughan went to Leeds University and every year they had a 'Rag Week'. My husband and I always went into town on the Saturday. There was a parade of students dressed in all sorts of costumes and a magazine was on sale. They also had a show at Leeds Empire and there Frankie did his first show. We saw him doing his turn with his straw hat and cane, never thinking how famous he would become. He took his name Vaughan from something his grandmother, in her Russian accent, said, "One ('von') day you will go far."

However, in Frank's own words, this how it really happened.

"We were looking for a name because my manager didn't think Abelson sounded or looked right on the bill heads. It didn't sound like a pop singer of the day – Frank Abelson. When he asked me my mother's maiden name that might do, her name was Cossack, that also sounded very strange. We couldn't imagine the young ladies shouting out Frankie Cossack and we were in dispute about it. My grandmother, I could hear in the background, I was on the phone to the family, and my sisters were screeching over the phone

"Frank's in show business and he's topping the bill and they don't have a name for him." My grandmother said, "It doesn't matter what they call him. For me, he'll always be number 'von', whatever he'll do, he'll always be number 'von'."

And from that moment on, the name Frankie Vaughan was born.

It is absolutely correct to say that Frank would have been number one in whatever line of work he'd have chosen to do. His abundant energy and unbridled enthusiasm would have made sure of that. But having once been described as possessing the looks of Victor Mature, the voice of Al Jolson and being Britain's answer to Frank Sinatra, Dean Martin and Tony Bennett all rolled into one, it was blatantly obvious that his rise to fame and fortune would undoubtedly be achieved through his unparalleled career in show business.

Right from the very start to the very end of his chosen profession, Frank, every step of the way, picked up one award after another, each of which was truly and richly well deserved.

As early as 1957 Frank was acclaimed "Show Business Personality of the Year" quickly followed by being voted a winner in a poll to find the "World's Outstanding Musical Personality" by readers of the New Musical Express.

In 1960, whilst in the USA, he was awarded the "Golden Microphone" by the International Sound Institute, the first British artiste to be so, ranking alongside the likes of Bing Crosby, Frank Sinatra, Sammy Davis Junior and Marlene Dietrich.

In 1965 he received the "Order of the British Empire" from the Queen for his services to the nation's youth and three years later became the youngest President yet of the Grand Order of Water Rats, the world's largest and most famous showbiz charity.

In 1993 Frank was appointed by Her Majesty the Queen, the Deputy Lord Lieutenant of Buckinghamshire and in the same year, scooped a "Lifetime Achievement Award" in the Liverpool Echo's Scouseology Awards.

The honours continued. In 1997 he was awarded the "Gold Badge" at the Savoy Hotel in London by the British Academy of

Songwriters, Composers and Authors. Once again he was elected by his fellow professionals to be 'King Rat' and, as the Vice President of the National Association of Clubs for Young Persons, the Queen created him a "Companion of the British Empire."

In 1998, the year before his death, he was made an Honorary Fellow of Liverpool John Moores University and also received a "Special Award" at the Liverpool Echo's Arts and Entertainment Awards.

But the highest accolade of all came from his wife of 43 years, Stella, when she had the following words inscribed upon his headstone,

"Mr. Moonlight – He enriched our lives."

Frankie Vaughan, Requiescat in Pace.

Forever a Star

The stars in their courses

shine brightly and warm

Their brilliance brings

comfort until a new dawn

Darkness enlightened,

a legend lives on

Celebrating the life of

Frankie Vaughan

JIM FINN,
2005